THE VALLEYS AUTOBIOGRAPHY

2

THE TIME OF OUR LIVES

VALLEY
CWM A BRO
&VALE

*A PEOPLE'S HISTORY OF THE
GARW, LLYNFI AND OGMORE VALLEYS*

EDITED BY C.M.KELLY

ACKNOWLEDGEMENTS

We are grateful to all the people who have shared both their personal recollections in the form of recorded interviews and their much-valued photographs and time in the creation of
THE VALLEYS' AUTOBIOGRAPHY 2: THE TIME OF OUR LIVES.

Kitty Bishop
Charles Bateman
Selwyn Bevan
Betty Blake
Alex Bowen
John Brain
David Brown
Elizabeth Cabble
Nancy Chilcott
Vernon Chilcott
Margaret Davey
Darren Dobbs
Warren Dryden
Doreen Evans
Vernon Evans
Bill Gibson
Christian Hoad
Jack Holt
Bernard Ingram
Jill John
Violet John
Bertie Jones
Megan Jones
Graham Jones
Gwennie Jones
Gwyneth Lewis
Merlin Maddock
Alison McGann
Gareth John Morgan
Grafton Radcliffe
Ivy Randall
David Rees
Ian Read
Elizabeth Roach
Councillor Wayne Sherlock
Michael Thomas
Will Trigg
Brenda Webster
Megan Wheeler
Garw Valley Summer Scheme Photography workshop

You can contact Valley and Vale Community Arts at:
Blaengarw Workmen's Hall
Blaengarw
Bridgend
CF32 8AW
Tel: 01656 871911
Fax: 01656 870507

FACTS is an award winner under the Pairing Scheme (the National Heritage Arts Sponsorship Scheme) for its support of Valley and Vale Community Arts' The Valleys' Autobiography 2: The Time of Our Lives. The Pairing Scheme is a Government Scheme managed by ABSA (Association for Business Sponsorship of the Arts).

FACTS

FACSIMILE & COPIER TECHNICAL SERVICES

01222 - 342424

INTRODUCTION

The Ogwr Valleys of Garw, Llynfi and Ogmore have, over the past one hundred and fifty years, shared an almost identical experience. Essentially rural valleys with a few small hill farms, by the mid nineteenth century the 'coal rush' engulfed them as it swept across South Wales. Industrialisation and mass migration ensued as thousands answered the call of an industry which would change the face of the land as well as the lives of the people.

One hundred and fifty years later, what it leaves behind is as important as what it brought with it. With the decline of the economic basis of these communities and with the rise of a modern passive culture which is largely imported, those forms of communication which shaped the collective memory are being eroded. This book is part of the process of people reclaiming their own histories and, having done so, beginning to shape their lives in the present and plan the sort of society they wish for the future.

The Valleys' Autobiography Project was launched at Maesteg Town Hall in 1991 in a major exhibition and is essentially a collection of life stories from the Ogmore, Garw and Llynfi valleys made possible by the generous assistance of **Ogwr Borough Council, the Welsh Development Agency, the Arts Council of Wales**, the **Business Sponsorship Incentive Scheme** and **Association for Business Sponsorship of the Arts**.

This publication is part of **The Valleys' Autobiography Project** established by **Valley and Vale** to record the memories and visions of the people of the valleys at a time of enormous social, economic and cultural change equal only to that during the exploitation of the coalfield which began less than two centuries ago. It is based on the premise that ordinary people are the only real experts in the histories of their own lives and that it is the apparently insignificant memories - the personal triumphs, the tragedies, the moments of humour and of pain - that tell us what it really means to live and work in the South Wales valleys.

Valley and Vale's involvement with the history of the Ogwr Valleys began in 1983. We work in a number of ways; we collect and copy people's photographs and record the details that go with them. We encourage people to recall their personal memories, the changes they have seen and their hopes for the future on to video. In addition, workshops for all ages are held in photography, video, music, dance, drama and design to promote active involvement by all the community using the photographic and literary raw materials gathered. In these ways, the products of **The Valleys' Autobiography Project** form a body of work which not only preserves but also makes available to others the discoveries that local people are daily making about where they live and where they came from.

The context in which we speak is as much a part of the history of our lives as are the events which we relate. In the telling of the story we become part of it. **The Valleys' Autobiography 2: The Time of Our Lives** is the second in a series of people's history publications produced by **Valley and Vale** and is part of the process of retaining the qualities and values which make the valleys communities distinctive, drawing strength and support from them and above all passing them on to those for whom they are even less than a memory.

Valley and Vale
1997

1

RECLAMATION

Top lake, Blaengarw 1997.

Oh the air is cleaner, the air is cleaner! You imagine now, years ago in the 1920s and 30s all the collieries working, pounding out all that dust and dirt. Mam would put her washing up on the line and when she'd go to fetch it, it was almost as damn dirty as when she'd put it out you know. The dust, especially in the summertime, the wind used to blow it down the valley - clouds of the damn stuff - Good God!

Bill Gibson
b.1920, Ogmore Vale

Nantymoel 1997.

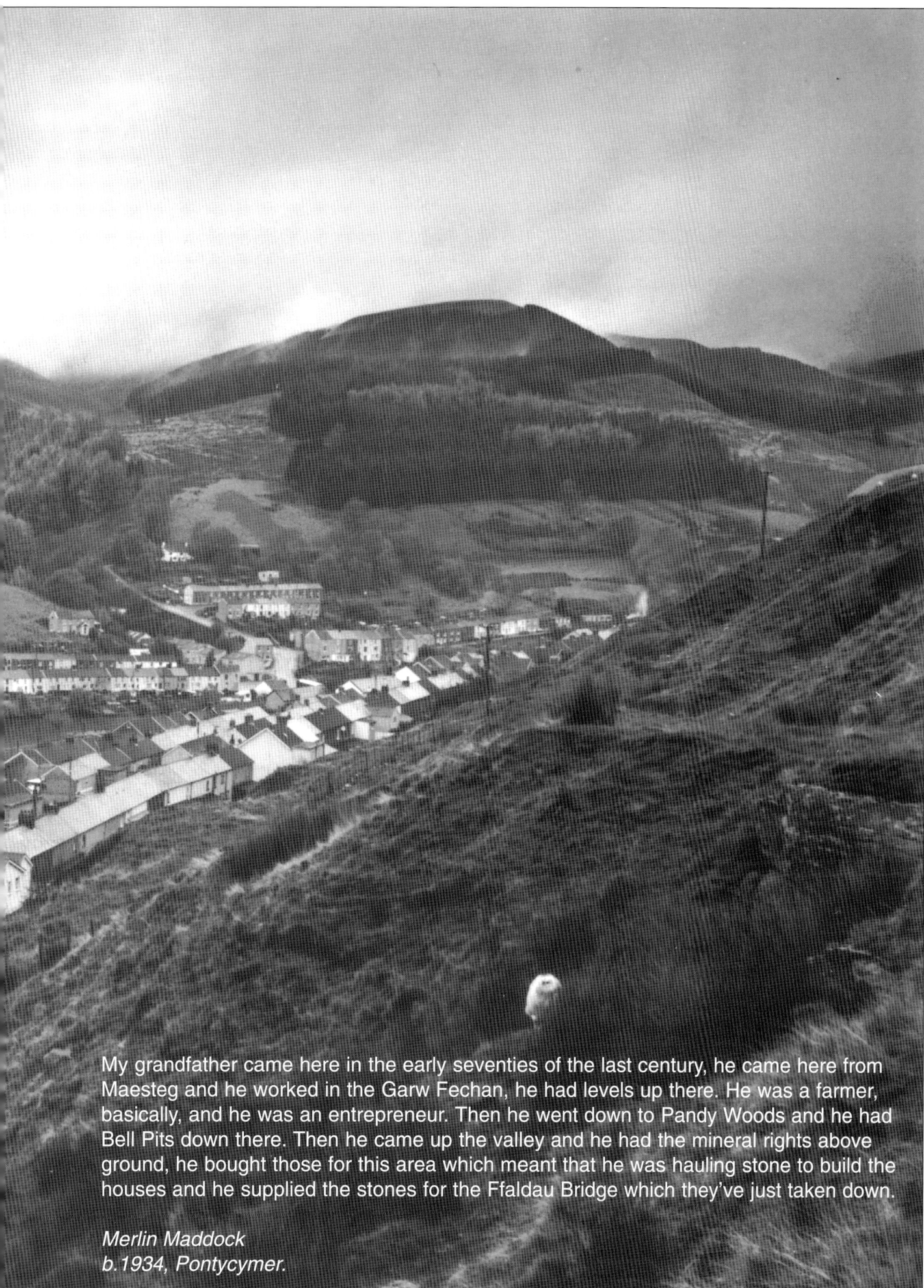

My grandfather came here in the early seventies of the last century, he came here from Maesteg and he worked in the Garw Fechan, he had levels up there. He was a farmer, basically, and he was an entrepreneur. Then he went down to Pandy Woods and he had Bell Pits down there. Then he came up the valley and he had the mineral rights above ground, he bought those for this area which meant that he was hauling stone to build the houses and he supplied the stones for the Ffaldau Bridge which they've just taken down.

Merlin Maddock
b.1934, Pontycymer.

Since the war, I was nursing and I met a lot of people from the Ogmore Valley, the Maesteg Valley and they seemed to be all entwined together, the valleys seemed to be.

Elizabeth Roach
b.1921, Nantymoel

Llynfi Valley looking down from Croeserw 1997.

Nantymoel 1997.

You know, the Ogmore and Garw are like sisters or brothers see. Innit funny now, Maesteg is the other one, that's alright but the Ogmore and Garw seem to be the same sort of person see.

Bill Gibson
b.1920, Ogmore Vale

To me, it's home. As my husband used to say, as you come up from Blackmill towards the valleys there was nothing like it, it's beautiful, the mountains and everything, it's really beautiful you know. There's something about the valleys that you don't get anywhere else because I've been away quite a bit and I met people but when you come back to the valley there's something about it that you want to stay, it's home. If you were born in the valley that's the place you want to die.

Elizabeth Roach
b.1921, Nantymoel

Bertie Jones and friends, Suffolk Pond Ogmore Vale 1930.

11

The new lake, Railway Terrace, Blaengarw 1997.

Where the collieries was they've grassed that over now and it's looking good, it's good. I'm glad all the collieries are closed because I wouldn't like to see a son of mine or even my grandson now, he's twenty two this year, have to go down the pit at fourteen. We went because we didn't know no different; there was nothing else for you.

Charles Bateman
b.1922, Nantymoel

View of Blaengarw from Darren Bungalows 1997.

Can they ever imagine what it would be like working in two foot six or two
foot nine, lying on your stomach all day and think and the roof going to
come down on you. Claustrophobic. No child born in fifty years time would
understand what it is to go underground, no child would. I went underground with my father at the Wyndham, I never worked underground -
he wouldn't let me go near it.

Merlin Maddock
b.1934, Pontycymer

James Evans ('Jim Bake') conductor
of Nantymoel Children's Choir when
a 13 year old pit-boy c.1903.

Garw Valley from Blaengarw Farm 1997.

Oh, it's changed tremendously. When the pits were here everything was so grubby, now every-thing is so lovely and clean and it looks so nice you know, it's a pleasure really. I remember it as a little girl being very dirty but today it's a pleasure to go for walks in the valley. It is beautiful.

Elizabeth Roach
b.1921, Nantymoel

We used to look out onto a large slab of concrete and you could see little up on the hillside. Now we look out we can just make out the lakes, the people up there, we can see the buz-zards hovering and a bit of wildlife around and it's a total transformation!

Ian Read
b.1961, Blaengarw

It is a beautiful place to visit, lovely walks, lovely hills. The valley is very beautiful, it's a damp, grey day but you will notice that unlike most of the South Wales valleys this one is very wide and the hills are not steep, they are beautiful hills. Garth mountain, I love looking down it, I see it every day as I walk home and it is very beautiful, very protected.

Jill John
b.1932, Maesteg

Well I think it's wonderful, the reclamation work, I think that this will be what my granny said when she came here and remembers the squirrel going from the bottom of the valley to the top. I think that would be lovely.

Merlin Maddock
b.1934, Pontycymer

Site of the old Caerau Colliery, Llynfi Valley 1997.

2

"THOSE WHO WORE SUITS TO WORK WERE IN A CLASS OF THEIR OWN"

Old Dick Shattock in his working clothes, 1930s.

We've had professors, doctors, a queen's
physician born in Pontycymer and the chap
that wrote 'Calon Lan' lived in the old
paper shop - and May said they've got me!

Will Trigg
b.1909, Blaengarw

Over one hundred years there's been coal mining in the Garw and millions of pounds have been made. Everything in the Garw - miners built it, a penny a week out of miners' welfare for the Hall, pennies a week for the doctor...

Will Trigg
b.1909, Blaengarw

International Colliery, Blaengarw c. 1920.

Miners on man-riding spakes, Bryn Chwith c.1940.

I went down the mines at fourteen. There was nothing else you could do - you followed your father, your brother. There was two collieries up in Nantymoel, the Wyndham Colliery and the Ocean (before it became the Western Colliery it was the Ocean Colliery). Now, I went up to the Ocean Colliery to start and they wouldn't start me because I was too small so I went to the Wyndham Colliery which was just down the road not far away (they were only about a half a mile between each other) then they started me, they gave me a start there. They wouldn't start me in one because I was so small so then I went to the other one.

Charles Bateman
b.1922, Nantymoel

On 19th April 1937, I started work at the Ocean Colliery. My age was just 14 years. There was no pre-training. We went down in the cage and straight to the coalface. Some boys, with fathers or elder brothers already working in the pit, were lucky enough to be taken under their wing and shown the ropes. I had no one. Arriving at the pit-head, I was immediately befriended by a man named Ben Jenkins who took me into the cage, pointed out the iron bar to which I had to hold on tight as the cage dropped like a stone into the bowels of the earth. The sensation was not of going down, but soaring upwards as if in an aeroplane.

Grafton Radcliffe
b.1923, Blaengarw

Winding gear Wyndham Colliery, Ogmore Vale 1980.

20

You left school at fourteen, you was down the pit the following day and you worked as a collier boy then and sometimes, it all depends on who you were working with, you was having quite a jovial time in between the little breaks.

Will Trigg
b.1909, Blaengarw

Dinner break c.1910.

Will Bodenham was my first 'butty' - turned out to be a man with a heart of gold. Probably remembering the trauma of his own first day underground, he went through the ritual with great patience. The coalface itself I regarded with awe. All I could think of on contemplating that black, glistening wall, was that it had been there for millions of years. Now, we mere mortals were charged with hacking it into lumps of transportable size and sending it back to the surface. Coal was hewn using a variety of implements such as a sledge-and-wedge, an iron prising bar and pickaxes (called 'mandrils'). When a large enough pile of coal had accrued, the task of the boy was to load it into the tram. The nature of the coalface varied from stall to stall. In some, the coal was so hard ('like the hobs of hell') that a man could hack at it for hours and produce only a small amount. In others, the coal was so so easy to hew ('boiling out') that a man and boy could easiliy fill numerous trams. The latter then had a good wage packet on Friday, while the former, who had worked much harder, took home only the statutory minimum wage of two pounds five shillings.

Grafton Radcliffe
b.1923, Blaengarw

21

' *Sinkers' going on shift at Ffaldau Colliery, Pontycymer 1946.*

Well as you got older then, you come to a place of your own working as a collier, you had a collier boy with you and I always remembered some of the rough times I had with some different workmen and good times you had with others, so I had a conscience as far as the boys worked with me. They had to work mind!

Will Trigg
b.1909, Blaengarw

Ffaldau Colliery Coke Ovens, Pontycymer c.1910.

Miners who were householders received concessionary house-coal. It was a custom as old as mining itself. Because they went home dirty from the pit, had to bath every day and needed fires to heat the bath water and dry wet working clothes in readiness for the next shift, miners were allocated twelve loads of concessionary coal a year. The house-coal was delivered by Hughes 'the farm' and his sons. It was extremely hard work and not only for humans. The Hughes method of transport was horse and cart. As no one animal could have hauled ton after ton of coal per day up steep Blaengarw gradients, a team of horses, harnessed one behind the other in single file, had to be used. Getting a load up the precipitous approaches to, say, Tymeinwr Avenue, was a major operation. The horses first had to be galloped into the slope at full speed in order to get a start on the hill. Once there, they had to be kept going at all costs. The sight of these creatures careering up the incline in full flight, with the Hughes boys shout-ing, screaming, cajoling, bullying and generally spurring them on to even greater effort, only needed John Wayne riding shotgun to resemble a stagecoach sequence from some Hollywood western. Later, Hughes 'the farm' invested in a lorry. While one was glad for the horses sake, house-coal deliveries were never the same again.

Grafton Radcliffe
b.1923, Blaengarw

Working underground, details unknown.

My father worked in the 'Bala' and head to take dry clothes to work to change into twice a day. He had dermatitis in his legs from working in water.

John Brain
b.1938, Blaengarw

Tom Stephens, Griff Jones, Shoni Gool, Ogmore Vale 1930s.

I worked in the Ffaldau in 1945 and I worked on top first of all and then I worked underground - later mind. We were fed up with working on the surface in all weathers so we decided to go underground and ten shillings a week extra. So we went to a training school in the Rhondda and Ogmore and when I came back I was transferred from the Ffaldau to the Garw Colliery or the Ocean, everyone called it the Ocean, but I didn't like it there at all, it was a horrible pit to work in and I came out of there and I got called up for the army, for the National Service you know.

Bernard Ingram
b.1929, Pontycymer

Ocean colliers on nationalisation day, Blaengarw 1947.

I started in '54 and the International was converted from steam to electric. Nationalisation in 1947 was when everything started to get modernised. I was an electrician then and the men refused to go down on the first day of the electric winder because they reckoned it wasn't safe!

John Brain
b.1938, Blaengarw

After nationalisation, a Pit Consultative Committee was established, to which I was elected. Given the 'new era' of industrial relations that had supposedly dawned, the committee was expected to defecate wonders and urinate miracles. It did not work out that way. At meetings, held in the colliery office, representatives of the men sat at one side of the table, management appointees on the other, and the colliery manager, James Breacher, was Chairman. Our terms of reference stipulated that majority decisions were not allowed. We had to reach 'unanimous agreement'. In spite of nationalisation, the differences between men and management were as wide as ever. All the two sides did was argue and quarrel. No agreement, unanimous or other-wise, was ever reached and the whole exercise proved a waste of time.

Grafton Radcliffe
b.1923, Blaengarw

He was secretary of the Lodge for 28 years till the pit closed. He enjoyed it, it was a busy time but he enjoyed it. He was all for the colliers, they thought the world of him. Any trouble, they'd go to him and he always took it, he was good! I saw him one day, a chap come to him and he had a hundred pound cheque for some accident that he'd had and he said I don't think this is enough for what I suffered and out with his pen and he put another nought.

Brenda Webster
b.1909, Ogmore Vale

Fronwen Terrace, Ogmore Vale 1947.

The winter of 1947 when we had heavy snow I was working in Dyffryn Hall, the training school. We came up from the pit one day and the snow wasn't coming *down* it was coming *in*, horizontal. We managed to get on the bus as far as Cymmer and the driver tried to go up the hill and couldn't so we all had to walk up. We got up on the top, oh there was a gang of us, some from the Garw and some were from Ogmore Vale, and a furniture van came along, one of Herberts', and he stopped "Do you want a lift?" We all piled in the back, got to Maesteg, had a bus home and when we got up in the morning and looked out of the window the valley was white. We had four foot drifts of snow and nothing moved for about three or four days in that valley, nothing, no trains, no buses, no sort of transport and of course, the only way we could get to Dyffryn Colliery about a week or so later was by train and the hill going from Caerau up to the top, there were twenty foot drifts there. It took weeks to melt.

Bernard Ingram
b.1929, Pontycymer

27

We had a chap, he had a bad leg and he used to work in the Ffaldau. Jack Jones 'Lame' I think his name was because he was Jack Jones, lame. Then we had a chap called Tommy 'Bargoed'. Now, Tom came from Bargoed you see, he wasn't from the Garw but he lived in the Garw so he was Tommy 'Bargoed', see. Then there was Dai 'Small Coal', now he was working in the washery and he was clearing out the small coal, that was his job and so he was Dai 'Small Coal' you see.

Bernard Ingram
b.1929, Pontycymer

I married a miner and he worked there until he retired and he had that dust disease then.

Margaret Davey
b.1922, Nantymoel

Brynmenyn Colliery Rescue, c.1910.

When I was in the pit I had the unfortunate part of helping to dig out a relative of mine who got killed; about six months before I left the pit he got killed in the colliery. We had talked about it, my wife and I, must come out of the pit now... So I came out and I become a part-time postman, eventually come full-time postman and I stayed there until I retired.

Charles Bateman
b.1922, Nantymoel

Ffaldau Colliery Coke Ovens, Pontycymer c.1910.

Coalface, pit props and conveyor, location unknown 1980s.

In the Christmas of 1979 I took voluntary redundancy. I could see a totally different feeling coming into the pits, you know. The younger element, they didn't seem to care so much. As far as I was concerned my job was my living but the youngsters didn't seem to bother at all mun! I had a good job, I was on pit-bottom, I was there for maybe twelve, thirteen years. I had a nice little job but I was glad to finish. So I finished then and I decided "Well, that's it". I was sorry to see the pit close for the youngsters but they didn't seem to care, they weren't all that fussy but jobs are scarce now and quite a few have come up to me since and said that they were sorry to see the pits close.

Bill Gibson
b.1920, Ogmore Vale

Demolition of Ocean Colliery, Blaengarw 1986.

29

*Violet John,
member of
Womens Support
Group at
St. Johns Colliery,
Maesteg return to
work 1985.*

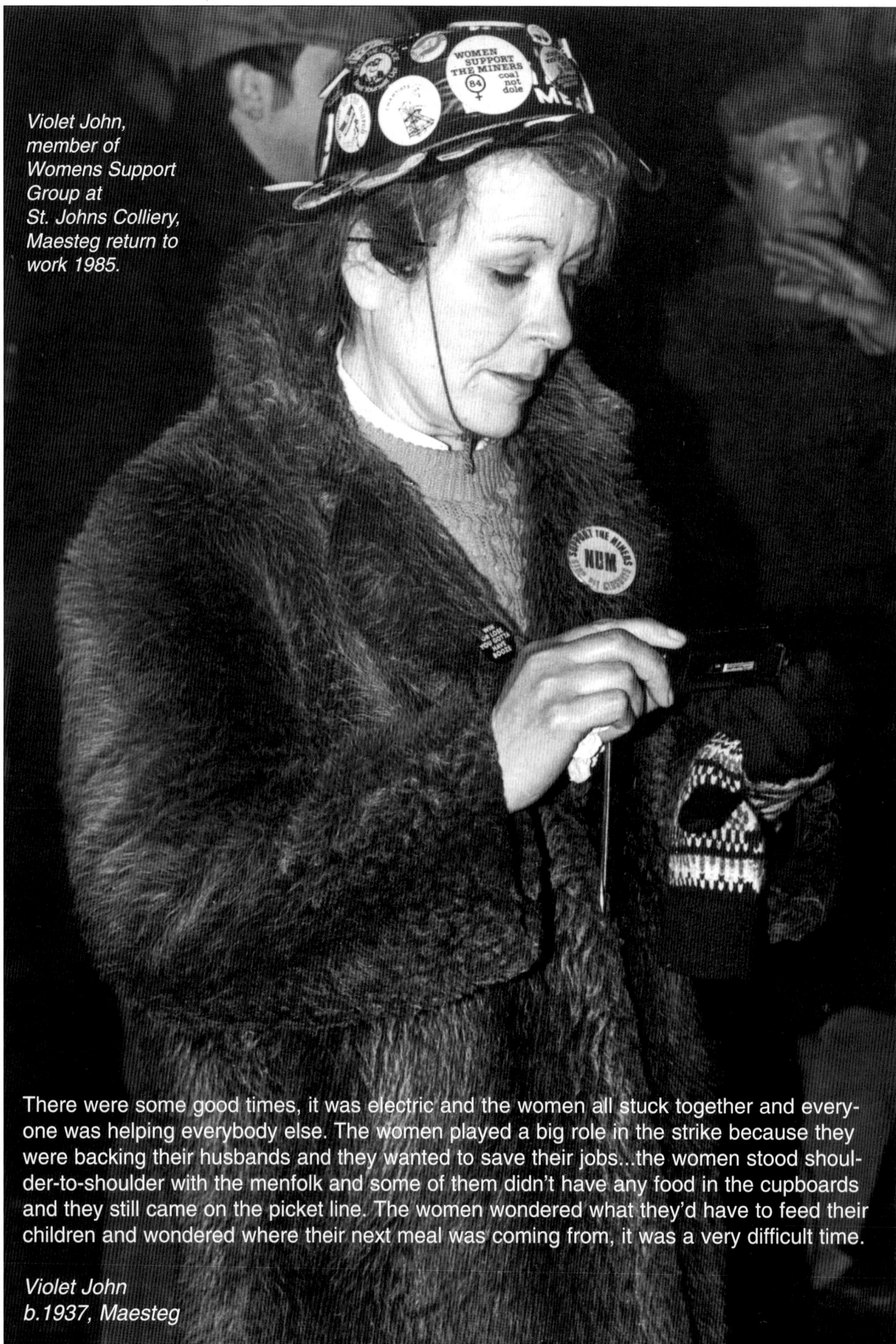

There were some good times, it was electric and the women all stuck together and everyone was helping everybody else. The women played a big role in the strike because they
were backing their husbands and they wanted to save their jobs...the women stood shoul-
der-to-shoulder with the menfolk and some of them didn't have any food in the cupboards
and they still came on the picket line. The women wondered what they'd have to feed their
children and wondered where their next meal was coming from, it was a very difficult time.

*Violet John
b.1937, Maesteg*

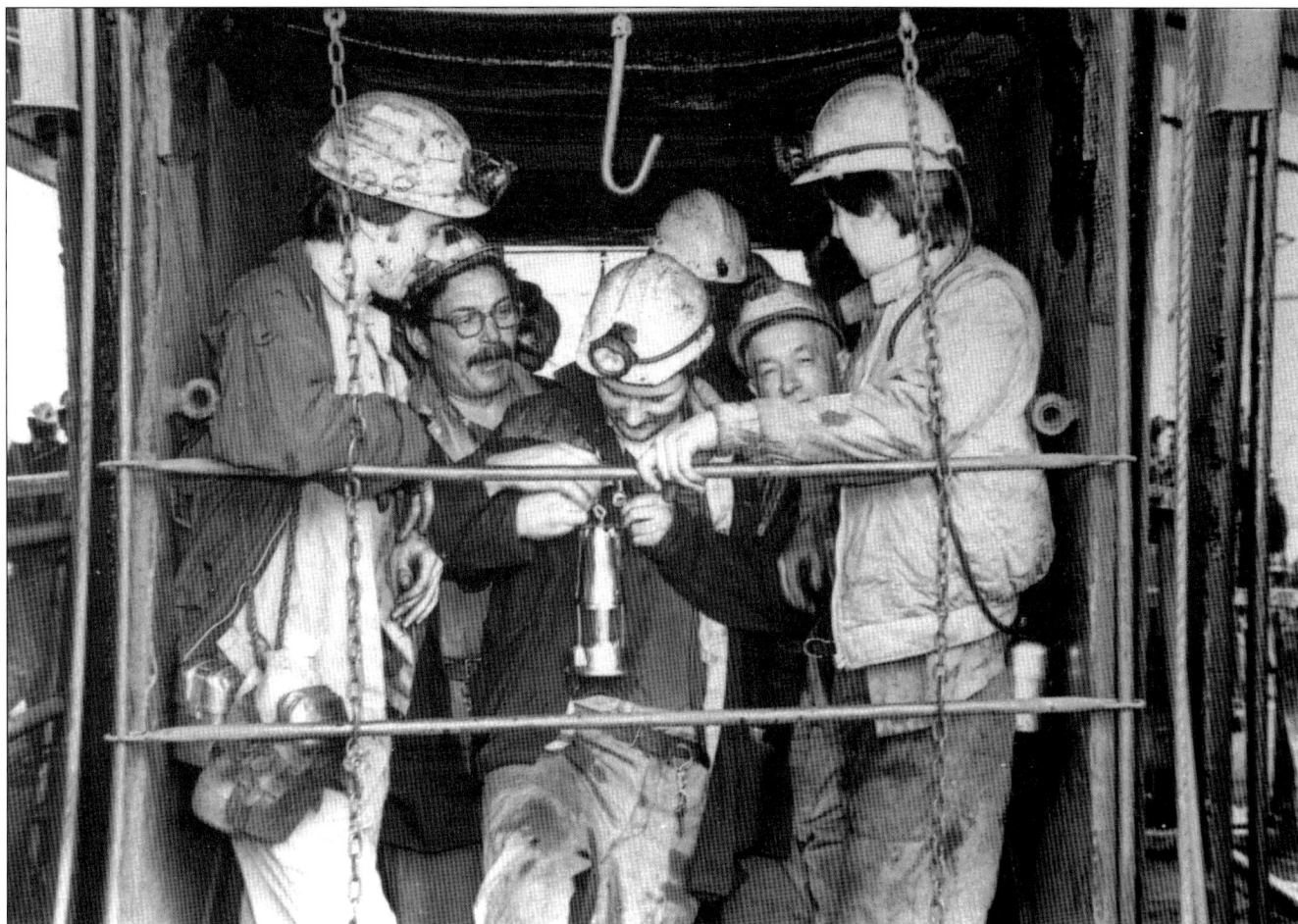

Men descending at St. Johns Colliery, Maesteg 1985.

There are no mines here. I suppose you are relieved in a sense that there are no mines in that you don't have the dreadful accidents, you don't see those. But having said that, I can understand my father when he talked about comradeship of people in the mines. There's not quite the same comradeship in a factory as there was with the mines and really you can see that there's a bit of 'hiraeth' for the mining industry.

Gwyneth Lewis
b.1926, Maesteg

The vicar asked me what'll be on my gravestone, like, and I said "The only thing that I do know what will be there 'cachu deryn'," that's Welsh, do you know what it means - birdshit!

Will Trigg
b.1909, Blaengarw

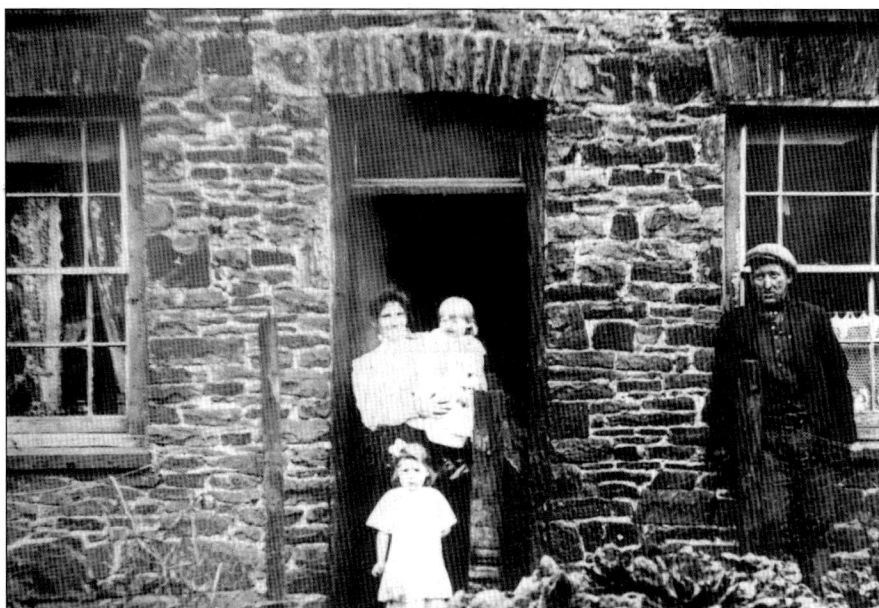

Family group, details unknown c.1920.

I don't remember much about my mother, I was only seven when she died. But my father, he liked his drink, I think he destroyed the home for that, he'd sell anything to have a damn sixpence for a pint of beer - that's how they were in those days, all booze. My grandfather was under-manager of the Wyndham Colliery and I had two uncles there and my father and my brother were colliers there. I didn't have any hopes at all. I had two older sisters, well by the time I was twelve they had both gone, married and gone , so I had the house to look after, my father and three brothers and I was only twelve. It was hard work.

Brenda Webster
b.1909, Ogmore Vale   *Four generations of the Walker family, Ogmore Vale, date unknown.*

For the daughters of the house life was usually one long domestic chore. While the men were able to find work in the pits there was virtually nothing for their sisters. A few lucky ones became trainee nurses, others went into domestic service in London working as maids to the wealthy for little more than their keep and some pocket-money; a few were accepted by local businesses as 'apprentices'.

Grafton Radcliffe
b.1923, Blaengarw

Two 'Mams', Ogmore Vale c.1930.

33

In 1939 I worked in a big house in Llantwit for a year. I had a pound a week, marvellous money and I didn't have to wear black stockings, it was a real thrill to be able to put a light pair of stockings on! In service you were treated like - less than the dirt.

Kitty Bishop
b.1917, Ogmore Vale

Marilyn in the kitchen of 12 Tynewydd Row Ogmore Vale, date unknown.

My father worked in the mines. I had two sisters, when they become fourteen they had to go away to work (your parents couldn't keep them so they had to go away) they went to service, they went up to England in service. One sister went up to Bath, went to a big house up there, like a maid or whatever you call it and she worked there and she would come home occasionally. My other sister then, she went away to work, then she went to work down outside Bridgend, Ewenny, on a farm down there because you had to, your parents couldn't afford to keep you, that's the reason I had to go underground at fourteen 'cause there was nothing else to do, you had to follow your father or your brother and work underground.

Charles Bateman
b.1922, Nantymoel

Another daily task for the ladies was 'emptying the slops'. With bedrooms being on the third floor and the lavatory located at the bottom of the garden, the needs of nature had to be satisfied at night by using chamber-pots, kept under the bed. The following morning they had to be emptied, washed and disinfected ready for the following night, another of the unpleasant tasks that daughters of the house, who were kept by their menfolk, had to perform without question.

Grafton Radcliffe
b.1923, Blaengarw

Bridgend General Hospital, Quarella Road 1941.

There weren't many things that you could do, there was either teaching, nursing or service. Service was out, teaching was out, so my father said "Well what are you going to do then?"
So I applied then to go nursing. I had a wonderful time, I wouldn't have done anything else. I nearly didn't get it because I conked out; they took me round and ooh it was terrible, shocking, and I passed out. I was taken and put in a side ward and they said if I couldn't do any more then of course, I wouldn't be able to continue. They showed me a gangrenous leg and I vowed then I would never ever treat anybody young as they treated me!

*Megan Wheeler
b.1921, Blaengarw*

Megan Wheeler behind Church Terrace, Blaengarw 1943.

35

My father was ill and I came home to nurse him and they asked me if I would take the post of District Nurse because the one that was doing it was having babies, she had twins. So after a lot of humming and hahing I did it, I nursed up here. I worked for all the doctors but I was more specially the miners' nurse because the miners paid for Doctor Rees as their doctor - I think they paid about sixpence a week and a couple of pennies a week for the nurse. The doctor and the nurse were the miners'. There was quite a number of doctors up here, Doctor Mac, Doctor Sadik, you name them all and I worked for them all!

Megan Wheeler
b.1921, Blaengarw

District Nurse Megan Wheeler with Gladstone bag, Blaengarw 1945.

He was a collier in the drift, Penllwgwent, and he was
an NUM man for 28 years, till the day the colliery
closed. I worked in the colliery canteen. We finished
work the same day - the colliery closed see. I've
worked all my life from the time I was twelve. When I
came thirteen or fourteen I met up with this boy and by
the time I was eighteen I was married and had a baby.

Brenda Webster
b.1909, Ogmore Vale.

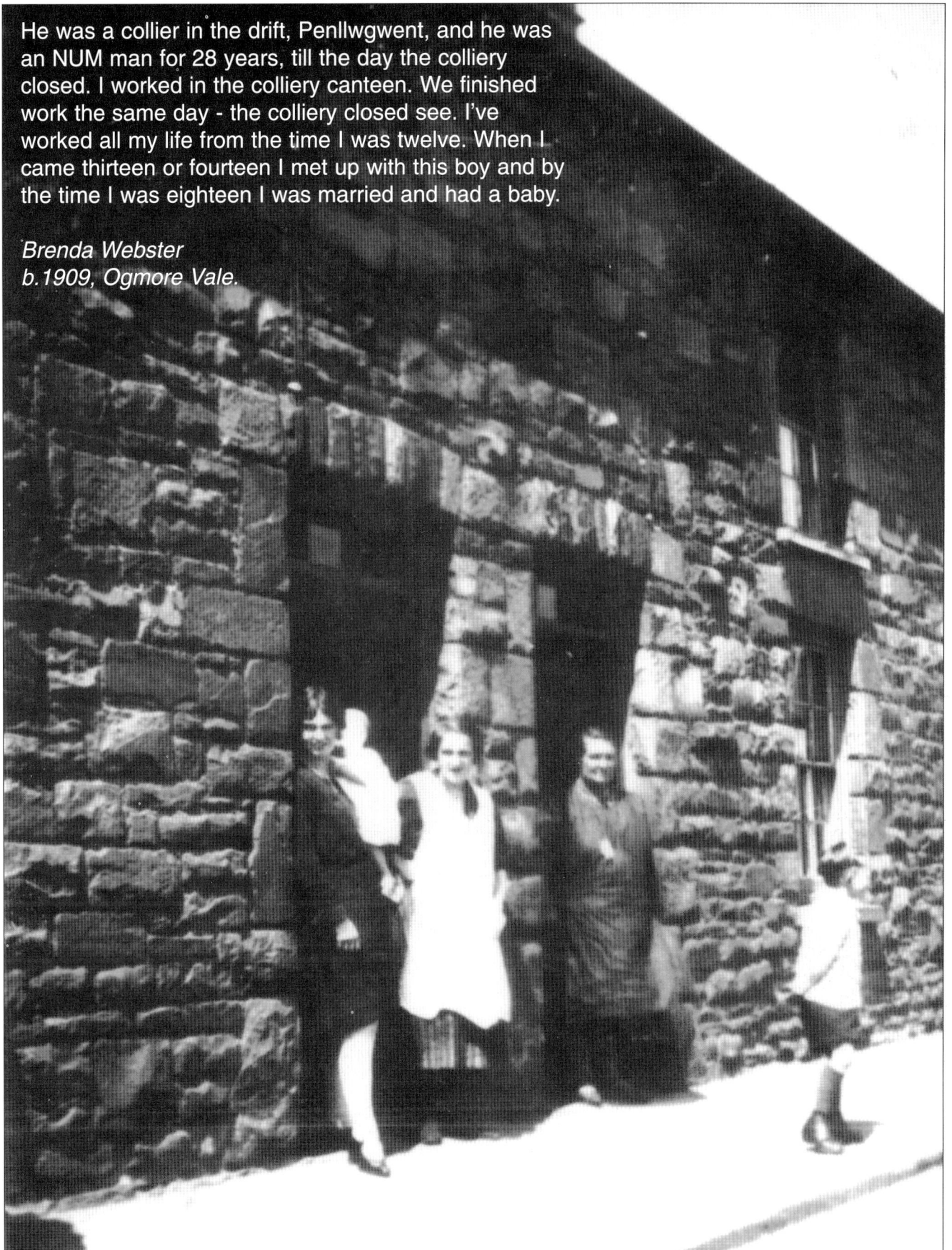

We was pushed aside; it was all male then, everything was in those days. Women didn't
take much part in the valley - one or two did - I mean, one or two went into politics. One of
my friends did, Lady May Lewis did, but of course that was quite a few years after.

Ivy Randall
b.1909, Blaengarw

Tynewydd Row, Ogmore Vale c.1928.

Ogmore Vale c.1900.

Miss Fannie M. Thomas was an important woman in the community in a day and generation when, with a few notable exceptions, men seemed to be far more prominent in local affairs and in the day-to-day conduct of business and commerce. Most streets seemed to have a quota of important men: sporting, political, cultural, religious, trade union; but there were no women doctors, bankers, preachers, police, solicitors, business leaders. Most women in the Garw were far too involved in bringing up large families on meagre wages, or on the dole, to be active in public life and at the same time maintain a high standard of cleanliness of home and family, with little or no facilities to ease the burden.
Miss Thomas was a torch-bearer for her sex in the days when you needed courage to do so. She was a woman before her time, intent on helping to blaze the trail for women's rights and opportunities. A passionate all-out worker and supporter of the Suffragette movement, she spoke of the cause with zeal and conviction.

Miss Thomas was one of the first women to be active in the political life of the Garw Valley, not only becoming the first woman member of the Ogmore and Garw Urban District Council, but later her all-male Council colleagues demonstrated their confidence in her by electing her the first woman chairperson of the Authority over sixty years ago.

While intrepid young women were daringly riding as pillion passengers on motorcycles that were appearing in greater number on British roads, Miss Thomas went a step further and bought a machine for herself, becoming one of the first motorcyclists in the Garw Valley.

Vernon Chilcott
b.1916, Pontycymer

In 1884 there was quite a sizeable population and the permanent inhabitants felt that they were being exploited by the local tradesmen so some of the men decided to call a meeting to see if they would form a Cooperative Society in order to supply goods to their members at a cheap and reasonable price. A meeting was held in the back room of the Coffee Tavern in Cardigan Terrace in Nantymoel and thus the society was formed. The minimum shareholding was five pounds and after a house-to-house canvas the initial fifty persons were recruited in a very short time. The first shop was a zinc shed in what is now Dinam Street in Nantymoel. From that date the society never looked back, eventually supplying everything to members from the cradle to the grave, they even gave free insurance to members and wives for funerals. They also built a modern new bakery in Nantymoel in 1911 and introduced pasteurised milk to the valley when they opened a pasteurised milk bottling plant in 1930.

Jack Holt
b.1918, Blackmill

Gwalia Stores staff, Ogmore Vale 1914.

You see, unfortunately, the only thing the committee of the Co-op was a bit behind with, 'till the late Fifties you had to leave when you got married. So that was my argument with the committee, "Look, we're training girls here, they're good girls, and once they get married they go and we're training them for other establishments". That eventually disappeared. It was a bit Calvinistic I think with, you know, the old Welsh Calvinistic principles.

Jack Holt
b.1918, Blackmill

Nantymoel Industrial Co-operative Society, Limited.

"Self Help." "Faithful in Co-operation." "Providence helps those who help themselves."

A GENERAL STATEMENT

OF THE

RECEIPTS & EXPENDITURE

FOR THE

FIRST QUARTER ENDING DECEMBER THE 28TH, 1885.

RECEIPTS.	£	s.	d.	EXPENDITURE.	£	s.	d.
To Contributions	238	14	0	By paid out for Goods	500	5	6
Propositions	3	5	0	G.W.R. Company	11	9	4
Rebuts	0	12	0	Salaries	21	14	6
Received for Goods sold	346	0	7½	Refunded to Members	7	13	2
				General Expenses	2	18	5½
				Stationery	1	1	2
				Haulage	1	5	3
				Fixed Stock	35	16	1½
				Cash in hand at end of Quarter	6	8	1
Total	£588	11	7	Total	£588	11	7

LIABILITIES.	£	s.	d.	ASSETS.	£	s.	d.
To Members' Shares	238	14	0	By value of Fixed Stock	35	16	1½
Reserve Fund	0	5	9	Stock-in-trade	219	10	9½
Due to Creditors	0	0	0	Cash in hand	6	8	1
Dividend for the Quarter	22	15	3				
Total	£261	15	0	Total	£261	15	0

	£	s.	d.	
To Goods bought by Members	303	9	10½	Average of Shares, £4 15s. 5¾d.
Non-Members	42	10	8½	Number of Members, 50.
Total	£346	0	7	Dividend in the £, 1s. 6d.

The Shop will be closed on Tuesday, April 6th, 1886, to make up the books, and every Member is requested to clear up all accounts before that day.

All members with their capital under £5 are requested to pay their Quarterly Contributions not later than March 23rd, 1886, and any member not complying with the above will lose his dividend for the quarter.

The Quarterly Meeting will be held at the Coffee Tavern, Nantymoel, on Saturday evening, April 17th, 1886, when every member is requested to attend. Time of Meeting, 6.30 p.m. precisely.

Examined and found correct,

WILLIAM THOMAS, } Auditors.
JOHN E. JONES,

JOHN MORGAN, Secretary.

Sugar was scooped with a small shovel from a sack into one and two pound thick paper bags for the grown-up assistants to accurately weigh and then close the bags in a special way to ensure no leakage of the contents. For their weekend requirements of potatoes, the customers would have ready-prepared for them, seven and fourteen pound bags. Butter, margarine and lard would be kept on trays on a marble slab, and customers' requirements would be cut from the veritable mounds, with unerring accuracy.

Vernon Chilcott
b.1916, Pontycymer

Pontycymer Cooperative Society was the biggest in South Wales. They had twenty two branches, it was the biggest, oh yes, it was busy. They had their own mechanics looking after the transport and things like that, you know, and they had a bakery in Meadow Street and then they had the slaughterhouse in Pantygog.

Bernard Ingram
b.1929, Pontycymer

Commercial Street, Maesteg c.1900.

The Pontycymer Cooperative Society (annual retail sales once reached the million mark, earning the title 'The Millionaire Co-op') played a significant part in the business life of Pontycymer and other areas [and] was involved in many aspects of valley life.

Vernon Chilcott
b.1916, Pontycymer

Talbot Street, Maesteg c.1910.

I left school at fourteen and a half years old and I worked in the town. I worked in what was a china, hardware etc. shop and I worked for Mr. Gutteridge for seven and a half years... Mr. Gutteridge said to me "Would you like to go as a manageress to my shop in Pontycymer?" and this is what I did. I had a lot of kindness shown to me in Pontycymer. I used to go on the bus in the morning and travel home at night. I used to have two bus journeys each way!

Gwyneth Lewis
b.1926, Maesteg

Commercial Street, Maesteg c.1960.

41

Near to our house, at 17 Herbert Street, stood my grandparents' bakehouse. Few people bought bread in those days. They made their own - anything up to twenty loaves at a time. Because the ovens in their own kitchens were too small for the purpose, there were a number of public bakehouses in Blaengarw, and it was one of these that my grandparents ran.
It had a large coal-fired oven capable of accomodating 300 loaves at a time. After these were loaded, the heavy iron door was closed and the bread left to bake for about one and a half hours. When taken out, the bakehouse filled with the aroma of freshly-baked home-made bread with which no modern commercially made variety can begin to compare. And the taste, when smothered in farmhouse butter, was out of this world!

Grafton Radcliffe
b.1923, Blaengarw

Tucker's bread van, Talbot Street, Maesteg c.1910.

One of the popular things in a miner's lunch was Welsh cakes. We made a lot of them. It was nothing for us to do about seven or eight hundred Welsh cakes a day! A Welsh cake is known locally as a 'pick', throughout South Wales I think. One of the stories that's told how the word come about was a woman who was very proud used to make different varieties of Welsh cakes, fruit Welsh cakes, jam, lemon curd, coconut ones, she'd make about half a dozen varieties and her husband was very proud of her and he always used to tell his mates, "Taste my wife's Welsh cakes," and he'd tell them, "Take your pick". And that's how the word 'pick' come about.

Vernon and Doreen Evans
b.1919, b.1925, Maesteg

Then there were the Italian Cafes, open at six o'clock in the morning to sell chewing tobacco to miners on their way to work, and not closing until midnight. Whenever there was a big fight involving Jack Petersen or another Welsh idol of the boxing ring, men gathered in those cafes to listen to the commentary on the owner's wireless. Very few had receivers in their own homes.

Grafton Radcliffe b.1923, Blaengarw

The Italians came and kept the ice-cream shops and they worked very hard because they were open from about five o'clock in the morning. They'd catch the miners going to work,

Norman Lewis and Lusardi outside Central Cafe, Nantymoel 1950s.

you know. Men would catch a bus from Cwmdu or Coegnant or somewhere and they'd usually have a fag and a cup of tea before catching the bus to go on a day shift. Of course, you know you wouldn't allowed to take cigarettes or matches to the colliery and, of course, they had a fag there and went to work. They were open then for the afternoon shift coming home which was eleven o'clock in the night and they'd stay open until twelve, one o'clock, you know.

Vernon and Doreen Evans b.1919, b.1925, Maesteg

The Italian Cafes made their own ice-cream on the premises. The recipe was a closely-guarded secret, the ingredients were not. Ice-cream was then made from fresh milk, double cream, the yolks of newly-laid eggs and caster sugar. It was pure and delicious unlike some of the vegetable fat concoctions of today.

Grafton Radcliffe b.1923, Blaengarw

They have been a feature of valley life always. Italian cafes were places where people spent a lot of time talking, they were meeting places as well as for food, they still are today. We had Agazzi's and Fulgoni's when I was growing up and now we have the Spagna family and the Tambinis.

Jill John b.1932, Maesteg

W.J. Dyer, Hairdresser, Blaengarw 1930s.

After I left school in the April it was about May when my father came home and he said, "I've got a job for you".
"Where?"
"In Frank Crates' Barber shop," down just above the Pontycymer Hall you know, the old cinema.
"Job there for you, apprentice".
So I went there in the afternoon and told the chap who I was. So my mother had to buy a white apron off him. The shop would open from nine o'clock in the morning and we closed at

six thirty with an hour for lunch and I was given the magnificent sum of five shillings, which is twenty five pence isn't it in todays? Then we closed at half past six but I'd be there perhaps after that, but if the salon was empty off you go. On Fridays and Saturdays we closed at eight o'clock on Friday and seven o'clock on a Saturday, but on a Saturday I had to stay there to scrub the floors - no extra pay.

Bernard Ingram
b.1929, Pontycymer

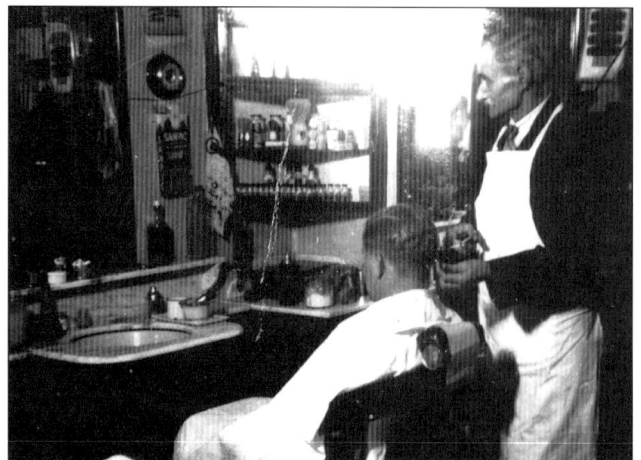

W.J. Dyer, Hairdresser (interior), Blaengarw 1930s.

Chimney sweep visiting Llangynwyd c.1900.

A postman by trade, Jimmy Beynon had some training as a dancer, at which he was very good. An extrovert by nature, he loved to stop and talk when on his rounds, and then proceed to give his listener a public demonstration of some intricate dance step, his postbag flapping against his backside as he did so...Harriet Anderson is another who springs to mind, taking around her horse and cart, ringing a handbell to let us know she was there, and selling parafin oil for the lamps that illuminated our homes.

Grafton Radcliffe
b.1923, Blaengarw

Katie Street, Blaengarw 1920s.

There were French onion-sellers who were quite a feature of this valley, they still come over but they used to stay in the Garth Inn for the months that they were here. One of my uncles actually went back with them one year and spent a holiday in the 1930s with them at their place in Brittany.

Jill John
b.1932, Maesteg

The Breton onion-sellers, known as 'Shoni Wniwns' called weekly carrying strings of the vegetables tied to a long pole resting on their shoulders. I remember one of them coming to our house on a very wet day. As the poor man had on no coat, wore 'daps' and was soaked to the skin, my father invited him in to dry out and have a meal. As they ate, they talked, my father in Welsh, the onion man in Bretonese, and both making themselves understood. Such are the similarities in the two languages.

Grafton Radcliffe
b.1923, Blaengarw

46

I still recall the cockle women from Penclawdd who went selling from door to door while balancing heavy wooden tubs of the shell-fish on their heads.

Grafton Radcliffe
b.1923, Blaengarw

Caerau Road, Caerau c.1910.

There was a woman who used to come up here, she was quite old but she had a big thing of cockles on her head, she used to carry them on her head. Then there was a lorry that used to come up with cockles. That was the night you shut the door and don't let anybody in! You buy them by the bucket, you see, and then my mother would clean them for about two or three nights to get all the sand and the salt out and then cook them over the range and when you'd hear them opening you'd have soup plates and bread and butter and eat them. No knives or forks, just go slurp! What was left, the juices, a little bread and butter and dip it in and you locked the front door so that people wouldn't come in and see you eating.

Megan Wheeler
b.1921, Blaengarw

3

"WE WERE ALL IN THE SAME BOAT"

Walters Road, Ogmore Vale, date unknown.

I went down King's Road and there was, what's his name? Dressed in black. Mosely, Oswald Mosely. I didn't know what they were, there were all these men dressed in black and I seen him marching and I said to the cook, "I've seen this man", I said,
"Aye, Mosely" she said, "Well, there'll be a war in about a twelvemonth now, sure to be," she said, like that. So I thought, quietly, 'Well, I'm going to edge my way back to the valley,' which I did do, which I did do.

Gwennie Jones
b.1919, Nantymoel

Wyndham Colliery, Ogmore Valley c.1920.

In 1939 came the war. Because coal was a vital wartime commodity miners were exempt from military service and not even allowed to volunteer for the forces. The only exceptions to this rule were flying duties with the R.A.F. and the Marine Commandos, two branches of the service where the mortality rate, as well as the required level of ability, were so high that suitable recruits were welcomed, no matter from what occupation they came.

Grafton Radcliffe
b.1923, Blaengarw

I went join the R.A.F. when the war broke out. I went to Cardiff, I had my usual medicals but because I was working in the mines I was turned down. That's right, I had my calling up, they turned me down because I was working in the mines and then later on I got a bit fed up working in the pit and I tried again but they wouldn't have me. I was on the coal, I was a coal-cutter so I wasn't allowed to go.

Bill Gibson
b.1920, Ogmore Vale

I went on the 14th of August 1939 and then war broke out in September. It was a workhouse [Bridgend General Hospital] but they emptied it because there was no-one there under about sixty you know up to about eighty or ninety, then they emptied all that because we were made a hospital for taking soldiers.

Megan Wheeler
b.1921, Blaengarw

50

Nurses filling sandbags, Bridgend General Hospital 1939.

I remember the day that war broke out, there was a public notice on the radio and on loud-speakers that all available youngsters should report to the market square in Maesteg on the Monday morning (war was declared on Sunday September the third). We went along to see what we could do to help. The idea was that we should fill sandbags to protect all the important buildings in the town such as the hospital, the police station and what have you, and we weren't filling sand we were filling coal slag from the tips and lorries were bringing this coal and tipping it into what is now the bus station area in Maesteg. We were actively filling these sandbags and a number of people who were unemployed came to help. We worked feverishly of course to fill these sandbags and I remember at the end, by Tuesday afternoon, our enthusiasm was such that we filled enough sandbags to cover Maesteg and we were all signed off and a number of unemployed men at the time were blaming us for working too hard and said that we'd work ourselves out of a job. And we did, we finished the work in two days and we went along and collected our pay which was one shilling and three pence an hour. But the men who were unemployed lost money that week because they had to put in three days waiting now before they could go back on the dole again and I think they were deducted the stamp for that week so instead of getting their normal unemployment pay, although they'd worked for two days, they were actually worse off at the end of the week. I always remember that story.

David Rees
Maesteg

On night duty you'd see rats running across those sandbags -
dirty big ones like cats they were!

Megan Wheeler
b.1921, Blaengarw

Bridgend General Hospital, Quarella Road 1939.

We were allowed to get exempted from 'call-up' until we'd completed our studies and qualified. I remember sitting my final examinations in June 1940 and finishing my examinations on one day and then reporting to the YMCA on the following day and I was in the Airforce and that was it. And sending my clothes, my civilian clothes, home by post because I wasn't even allowed to come home to say goodbye to my family. You were in and that was it! And you remained then until, well I spent five and a half years in the Airforce and fortunately survived. A lot of my friends didn't of course.

Jesse Mitchell from Maesteg 1940.

David Rees
Maesteg

Dilwyn Jones from Nantyfyllon c.1941.

Home Guard, Ogmore Vale 1940.

I was nursing in Aberdare, nursing in the military hospital in Cardiff and of course there was no choice, we either had to go nursing or join the forces or go to the ammunitition factory that they had in Bridgend which a lot of people did.

Elizabeth Roach
b.1921, Nantymoel

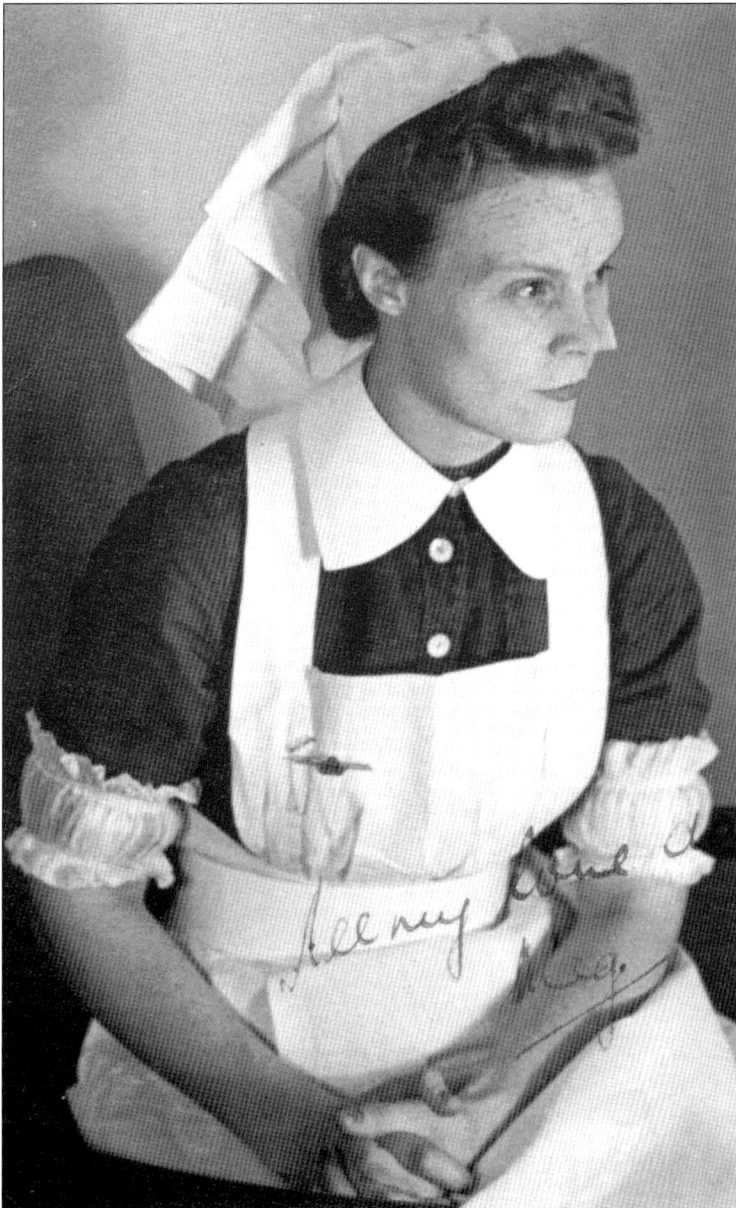

Megan Wheeler from Blaengarw c.1945.

We were conscripted, I was eighteen and of course we had to go away but it was lovely to come home afterwards. I was nursing. But the war years were very interesting, very, very sad but very interesting. That's something you'll never have again I don't think. People were for you, everything you did and there was a lot of respect in those days, which isn't today, there isn't the respect today that we had during the war years. Of course before the war things were different to what they are today, it was very poor, there weren't the jobs about. But today of course they've got everything but there isn't the same atmosphere.

Elizabeth Roach
b.1921, Nantymoel

I was one of the first, I think I was twenty, to have my call-up papers. So I saw Mr Llewelyn when he came home for lunch and I said "Oh, I've had my calling-up papers, I've got to go one day at the end of the week to Cardiff."
"What are you going to do?"
"Join the Air Force," I said, "I just want to join the Airforce". I'd been up in an aeroplane in 1934 from Rest Bay, small little aeroplane like Amy Johnson had, you know, and it was seven and six, a whole week's wages and I loved it. So I said, "I'm going to join the Airforce". So I went to Cardiff and they told me I couldn't join the Airforce because - that's when I found out. My mother used to say "You've got a cold on the chest, cold on the chest" but it was asthma, a bit of asthma. So I couldn't join the Airforce but I could join the army. Well, I didn't want to join the army so they said I can do war-work. I used to go down to Mr. Bert whose sons are still keeping the bakery in Brynmenyn, it was the Gwalia Bakery. I used to go down there once a week to help them make the bread and no wages. I stayed once a week all through the war.

Gwennie Jones
b.1919, Nantymoel

Bevan Boys, aye, now I was always sorry for them. I met them here myself. Young lads coming from London, no idea at all what the colliery was like, not the faintest. I know what it was like when I had to go down first, I had a rough idea but I was still frightened and to think of young lads taken from their homes - oh, I thought it was dreadful. They had to come down and they had no idea at all, poor little beggars, they had no idea, they probably would have gone to the army if they'd known, aye.

Bill Gibson
b.1920, Ogmore Vale

Group of school children in Ogmore's first bomb crater c.1941.

During the war I was in the fire service. I mean, that's part-time. I was working in the colliery then we'd go on duty two nights a week in a little shed and we had a lttle bit of a small fire engine, not a lot, one or two hydrants, well we didn't have a lot to do, very, very little. They done a good bit of bombing in Treorchy but we had nothing in the valley. Up in Nantymoel an aeroplane came down on the mountain but I was never involved in that at all like.

Charles Bateman
b.1922, Nantymoel

Soldiers, Ogmore Vale c.1939.

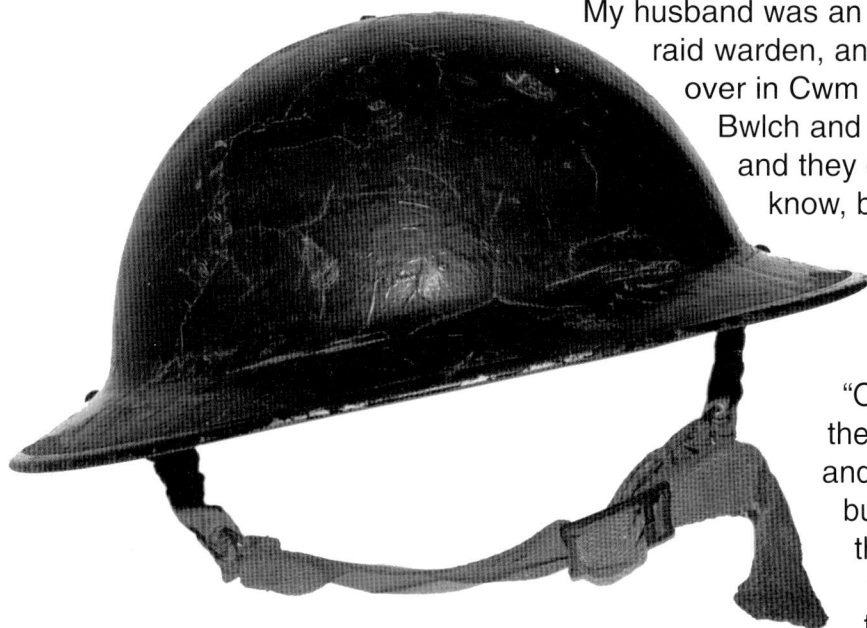

My husband was an A.R.P. warden, you know, air raid warden, and of course they dropped bombs over in Cwm Parc and we walked up to the Bwlch and we looked down over Cwm Parc and they dropped bombs up that way you know, behind Pembroke Terrace. Of course, he went out and, of course, he came home and he said "Look," he said, "I've burnt my gloves." So I said "Why?" "Oh well, I went to pick up one of them molotov bombs, you know, and it was still a bit hot like." and it burnt his gloves. So I said, "Huh, that's it," I said, "Well, you can do without gloves from now on then!" Course, they were given them by the A.R.P. you see. Well I said, "I'm not buying, it's the A.R.P. got to buy them and that's your lot!"

Elizabeth Cabble
b.1920, Nantymoel

My parents worked in the arsenal and there used to be a train for the afternoon shift used to come to the station in Pontycymer, three or four coaches and they'd be packed, it was packed with women on the platform, and a few men, of course. Apparently, there was about twenty thousand workers in each shift in the arsenal in Bridgend.

Bernard Ingram
b.1929, Pontycymer

There were people earning enough to be paid post-war credits from what they earned. A friend of mine worked in the offices of the arsenal during the war, her husband was a prisoner-of-war for the whole of the war and she made it her aim to save three hundred pounds by whatever time the war ended and she achieved that which was enough, of course, to buy a house to set them up when he came back. He came back in a very poorly state from his years in a prisoner-of-war camp in the Polish corridor near Trieste, but she had enough to set them up.

Jill John
b.1932, Maesteg

Tydfil Jones, Maesteg c.1942.

57

I remember the Yankies coming here alright. They camped over in the woods there the night. Scruffiest lot of fellows I've ever seen! And then they were giving the kids plenty of gum and tinned fruit and God knows what! Yeah, I remember them. And in the pubs they were, plenty of money, plenty of money they had, aye.

Bill Gibson
b.1920, Ogmore Vale

Pontycymer Station 1930s.

What I remember most is the war years. I remember the evacuees were sent to the valleys at the beginning of the war. I was coming home from school and I could see a train coming up the valley. Now normally when a train was coming in those days there were three coaches and one engine and there were six coaches and two engines so I thought, 'that's unusual'. So I got to school the following morning, when we got into the classroom there were all these drawings all over the boards. They had put the evacuees into the school and then they'd allocated them into their lodgings for people to come and pick them up. So to keep them occupied they'd given them chalk and they'd scrawled over everything.

Bernard Ingram
b.1929, Pontycymer

There was no shortage of people willing to take the children, poor little things. Imagine coming from London down here, didn't know what had hit them. But they loved it here, they used to have their mothers coming down then to see them, lots of people stayed here anyway.

Kitty Bishop
b.1917, Ogmore Vale

Well, of course, when the war broke then, we had evacuees living in our house...Fun...We had one very young, five, I don't know how old the other one was. We weren't going to have them and they all came and were put in the Church Hall when the train arrived. They were all there and they'd all got places except these two little ones. At ten o'clock at night they knocked on my mother's door and asked if she could take them in and what could you say? Anyway, we had them and, you know, it was fun because we used to fight over who'd get The Beano or The Dandy, you know, you're all young once again.

Megan Wheeler
b.1921, Blaengarw

Group of boys, High Street, Pontycymer c.1952.

Some of them were from Birmingham, some mostly from London and from the East End. No hills, no valleys and, you know, no fresh air, that's how they were brought up in the slums. They'd go walking down the streets and in those days there was only one colliery with pit-head baths and that was the Garw Colliery or the Ocean as we used to call it and of course most of the men coming from the pit had black faces. They had been underground and most of these children were frightened by seeing these men coming down, until they got used to it you see.

Bernard Ingram
b.1929, Pontycymer

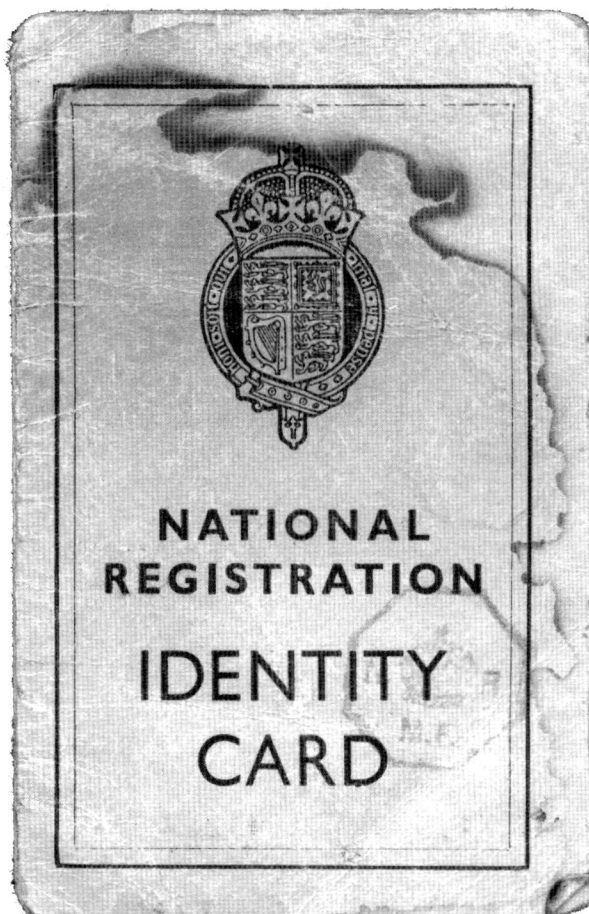

NATIONAL
REGISTRATION
IDENTITY
CARD

They were from London and they were treated as we were treated as children; they had a good home. The older one, I always think of watching my mother washing her hair on a Friday night and she said, asked "Auntie Maggie, are you afraid to die?" I don't know what my mother answered but she said, "Why? Are you afraid?"
"No, I'm not afraid of dying, I'm afraid of going alone."

Megan Wheeler
b.1921, Blaengarw

There was an outbreak of scabies and the thing to look out for was itching between the fingers, you know, and scratching. So the old St. John's Ambulance Hall which was on the square, they installed cubicles in there with a bath in each cubicle and you went in and they would paint your body with a paintbrush with a lotion that was in the bath, I don't know what it was, Lysol or something like that, carbolic. It stung, you know, but it did the job.

Bernard Ingram
b.1929, Pontycymer

Soldiers celebrate, Ogmore Vale 1940.

During the war, I attended a chapel service in a south coast town in company with a Maesteg friend. We were greeted at the door by a minister, a Welshman,
"Where do you come from?" he asked my friend,
"Nantyffyllon," was his reply.
"Say it again!" was the minister's enthusiastic response, "It sounds like music in my ears."

Vernon Chilcott
b.1916, Pontycymer

The rationing, two ounces of butter and I'd say come over and let's have one bloody good meal!

Brenda Webster
b.1909, Ogmore Vale

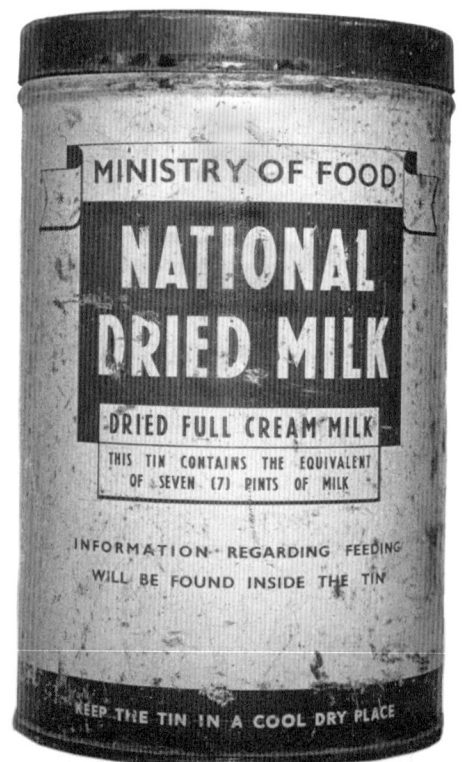

A feature of my life, because my younger sister was small then, was my Saturday job - to shop for my mother with the ration cards and queue for everything. Shopping was very difficult and waiting for the one orange you may be lucky enough to get or two bananas, anything extra that came into the town. But we lived quite healthily, my mother was a first-class cook and we certainly didn't starve. I do remember the joy if you could get a custard cream biscuit. We have so much of everything now that we don't realise what it's like to have a very rare treat of a custard cream biscuit or a tin of fruit. They were special treats reserved, possibly, for Sunday tea if you were lucky enough, or birthdays, people would save up for birthdays, and weddings and Christmas. But we did live healthily. Extra rations, of course, for mining families - extra cheese, because miners traditionally took cheese in their box to work, my father took cheese and Welsh cakes.

Jill John
b.1932, Maesteg

During the war years when we used to have a concert we'd send a pan, a dish around, or a bucket and people would put cigarettes and money in and we sent hundreds of pounds to the boys from this valley that were in the forces, you know.

Louise Thomas
b.1909, Ogmore Vale

George Mitchell from Maesteg and the Royal Army Service Corps c.1943.

The Avenue, Pontycymer c.1930.

They came here because they had a choice of going to the mines or to the army. The friendship that was made in those days they've still kept up in this valley, you know that, the Bevan Boys and the evacuees.

Kitty Bishop
b.1917, Ogmore Vale

61

Dick Lewis and Ceinwen, Ogmore Vale 1930s.

Wedding of Jesse and Tydfil Mitchell, Maesteg 1941.

Back in the forties there was a little place down the bottom of the valley, Cemetary Road, on a Sunday night now, that was a place where people used to be walking up and down. The boys that I used to play football with lived in Ogmore so I used to come down on a Sunday and we used to go strolling down that way. Now, two of them was courting but there was three ladies, three girls, that night and I was the odd man out and there was three girls so they said "Come on Charlie!" so we did and this one we met then is still my wife, and that was about 1941 I'd say, we got married in '45, we were courting a few years.

Charles Bateman
b.1922, Nantymoel

I was going out with an Italian boy in Ogmore but the war came and everybody in Ogmore said "Man, she's going out with an Italian, she can't go with an Italian!" and he was crazy on me but I wasn't crazy on him. People will know who I mean, his name was Joe Paccini and everyone was against it, that's because we were fighting them you see.

Gwennie Jones
b.1919, Nantymoel

Wedding group, details unknown 1940s.

I have a very clear recollection of the radio during the war. We used to have a map on the wall, a huge chronicle map of the world. It was in our kitchen above the radio and in the corner, at the side, it had pockets. In these pockets it had little flags with pins on and all the flags were a different nation. The German had a swastika, the American Stars and Stripes, British had the Union Jack and Australians had their flags. At four o'clock in the afternoon my father would be home from the Ffaldau Colliery, my grandfather would be home on Saturdays but not during the week. They would say the Germans are in Alexandria and they'd put the swastika flag, the British are now in North Tunis and they'd put the flag in there and you could see all the British and American troops coming in on Germany like you see those arrows in 'Dad's Army' today. That was marvellous, it was like a television on the wall. You know, when the news came on nobody spoke, you couldn't even eat a piece of toast to crunch, you know, they wanted to listen to the news.

Merlin Maddock
b.1934, Pontycymer

Troops returning from war 1945.

Tom Bara's soprano daughter, Megan, sang on the wireless. It was his singing that saved the life of her brother, Alford, when he was a Japanese prisoner-of-war. The camp commandant liked his voice so much that he kept him alive when all around, like the Thomas brothers of Katie Street, were dying like flies from overwork, starvation and brutal treatment.

Grafton Radcliffe
b.1923, Blaengarw

VE Day party, The Strand, Blaengarw 1945.

During the war, at the beginning of the war, there was a scare about gas attacks so everywhere you looked there would be a patch of green paint on these buildings you know, and when we found out what it was for, somebody said, "Well, that's in case of a gas attack"! Now, if that green patch turns yellow there's gas about. I mean, by the time you discovered that it is yellow wallop, you're gone! Oh, we laughed, and those green patches lasted for years and years.

Bernard Ingram
b.1929, Pontycymer

If you had a vivid imagination the war was far more impressionable upon you. The one story that I can't stop laughing at. I couldn't speak English and my aunts couldn't make out why, when they used to put me to bed, why they used to find me asleep on the windowsill in the front room facing up the valley. We were sticking these flags over Cairo, the Germans were heading towards Cairo. Well my grandfather came from Maesteg and I heard Cairo and I thought they were talking about Caerau and every night when I went to bed (and this went on for days) the Germans were advancing on Cairo. I would get to the window and I would sleep looking up at the aerial up the mountain waiting to see lights coming and the Germans coming over from Maesteg, from Caerau!

Merlin Maddock
b.1934, Pontycymer

65

VJ Day victory carnival, High Street, Pontycymer 1945.

HIGH STREET
V.J VICTORY
CARNIVAL
1945

4

"Money We May Not Have Had, But We Were At Least Rich In Other Things"

Blaengarw lads 1940s.

I came here thirty years ago, I came here for a wedding and I stayed because the people were so nice. I was living in Pontycymer then, mind.

Violet John
b.1937, Maesteg

Ogmore Vale Workmen's Hall, date unknown.

The chapels were centres of the community like the workmen's halls were and the clubs and the pubs were all centres for certain classes of people.

Merlin Maddock
b.1934, Pontycymer

All did spare-time study after working hours. All were helped by Blaengarw Workmen's Library which loaned them the books they needed and which their families were too poor to buy. Blaengarw Workmen's Hall ran university extra-mural classes in the Lesser Hall. On Saturday afternoons the building was always crammed with youngsters all eager to learn.

Grafton Radcliffe
b.1923, Blaengarw

T.C. Evans, The Bard 'Cadrawd', Llangynwyd c.1900.

The miners' libraries, the miners' institutes became a very important feature. They offered very good library facilities, very good quality books covering children's books as well, a lot of non-fiction too. They were very large buildings used for many purposes, they would have sporting facilities, a lot of boxing went on so they would often have a boxing gymnasium. They had debating rooms, they took the daily papers, they would have concerts there, rooms big enough to hold dances and big concerts. One former miner told me that his love of opera started in the miners' library with visiting artists coming.

Jill John
b.1932, Maesteg

Weslyan Chapel, Maesteg c.1910.

The Pontycymer Ambulance Hall, which had risen almost literally from the ashes of the celebrated Hippodrome Theatre, later known as the 'Rink' which was burned to the ground in 1922 in one of the Garw's most destructive fires, had not only been the headquarters of one of the most successful ambulance and nursing divisions, but had been an all-purpose venue for many kinds of events. Plays and pantomimes, dances and whist drives, horticultural and dog shows, lectures, discussions, meetings etc. - the Ambulance Hall, Pontycymer, had held it!

Vernon Chilcott
b.1916, Pontycymer

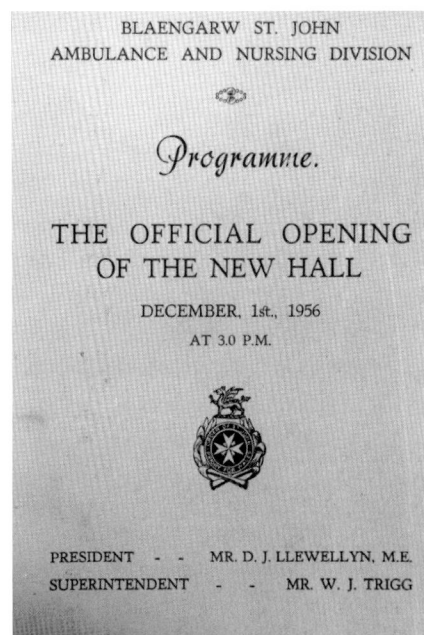

BLAENGARW ST. JOHN
AMBULANCE AND NURSING DIVISION

Programme.

THE OFFICIAL OPENING
OF THE NEW HALL

DECEMBER, 1st., 1956
AT 3.0 P.M.

PRESIDENT - - MR. D. J. LLEWELLYN, M.E.
SUPERINTENDENT - - MR. W. J. TRIGG

Oh, I've had as much as eighty on that stage in the hall, all different ages up from the small ones and I always remember my granddaughter. I was conducting that year, I wasn't acting in it, and she said "Nan, Lisa have peed on the stage!" and she came and she lifted her dress up and she said "I haven't wet my knickers Nan," all in the middle of the concert. Well, everyone went hysterical, I think they used to look forward to that more than the acting, you know. They were funny, kids are so funny, aren't they?

Louise Thomas
b.1909, Ogmore Vale

Cast of 'H.M.S. Pinafore', Blaengarw 1930s.

The Blaengarw Dramatic Society was one of the best in the country, and in considerable demand throughout South Wales. When they did a play the society toured widely and its productions often ran for a year or more. It was the golden age of drama. Every miners' welfare hall in every valley ran an annual competative 'Drama Week', with a different play by a different company performed every night and a final adjudication on Saturday. There were over a hundred such festivals a year in South Wales alone, including one at Pontycymer.

Grafton Radcliffe
b.1923, Blaengarw

One act in particular I remember watching with admiration and envy. A young man with a fifteen foot long whip carried out a variety of feats that left the audience gasping with astonishment when he whipped a cigarette from his partner's lips.

Vernon Chilcott
b.1916, Pontycymer

Nancy's father was very interested in fur and feather shows held in the Court Coleman Hotel. When he had these shows he used to wash the cockerels in the house and we all used to be in there helping him. My father kept chickens and all that but Mr. John was more interested in showing his cockerels.

Elizabeth Cabble
b.1920, Nantymoel

Poultry and Pigeon Society, Nantymoel 1909.

They used to have fetes down the village and the rugby field, oh marvellous fetes, and the maypole, oh it was beautiful. All stalls and prizes, oh they used to have fantastic fetes, it used to be wonderful, wonderful. I won a big bottle of champagne once down there and a pint and a half bottle of whisky with the draw. Oh God, I used to love fetes.

Gwennie Jones
b.1919, Nantymoel

Travelling Fair, Maesteg 1913.

We used to go as a family on picnics and we were a big family mind. My Gran had seven girls and then she had a boy and she always used to say she never made more of the boy.

Louise Thomas
b.1909, Ogmore Vale

We used to walk over to the Garw when we were little kids, you know. Take our little brown bag with our pack under our arms and go over the mountain, through the farms and come out on the top of the Ffaldau you know, by the cemetary by there. That's where we used to spend our holiday.

Elizabeth Cabble
b.1920, Nantymoel

Pantygog open-air baths, 1960s.

In the summertime we had the swimming baths in Pantygog, open-air swimming baths. You had cubicles, brick cubicles with a canvas cover. The deepest part was six foot going down to two foot or something like that. If you didn't have a costume you'd give fourpence and have one. It was fed through a stream that runs down there and in the summer it used to be full - it was practically ice-cold.

Bernard Ingram
b.1929, Pontycymer

74

Gang of boys, Tynewydd Row, Ogmore Vale c.1930.

We had 'whips and tops'. You could go down, there was a blacksmith living in Pantygog and he'd make you a wheel, you know, this round rod that he'd make into a wheel and a hook for it and off you'd go. We used to play a game on the way to school, follow your Tor. Now your Tor would be a fairly big marble or your favourite marble you see, and we'd play with the marbles along the gutter - in the gutter - all the way to school. Then you could hear the bell ringing so marbles in the pocket and off to school because if you were late you'd get a cane. If a teacher marked you late you'd have a cane and if you were very late he'd send you up to the head-master and you had a cane. Mr. Evans, I always remember, he had a thick cane on the side of his desk, the other teachers had a thinner one but, you see, the thinner cane gave you more of a pain because it stung.

Bernard Ingram
b.1929, Pontycymer

Some of the kids would bring old curtains into school and of course we'd be having weddings and God knows what when we were very young, see, we used to enjoy it.

Ivy Randall
b.1909, Blaengarw

Tymeinwr School, Pontycymer c.1910.

75

Boys from Blaengarw 1930s.

Our playgrounds was the colliery sidings and all the antics, you can never remember them all, but today, if I'd seen things happening today there, I'd have a heart-attack, all schoolboys playing with the electric and things on the collieries.

Will Trigg
b.1909, Blaengarw

Jimmy and Peggy Jones, Ogmore Vale c.1930.

What you'd do if you were lucky enough to get a comic, you'd go to one of your mates "Have you got this?" "No," well, swap your comics. Every Friday afternoon in school you could bring comics if you want to and read in the afternoon for an hour or two. We'd get comics and swap them on our own because we had good comics in those days, we had storybooks like The Wizard and The Hotspur, The Rover and things like that. There was such a variety of comics, you know, we lapped them up.

Bernard Ingram
b.1929, Pontycymer

We used to have happy school days. I remember we used to go to the pictures and our play-time was spent copying all the serials that were on at that time like Pearl White. Sometimes I'd land up as the idol stuck in the corner - they had outside toilets then with open windows - and I'd be sitting there all playtime cross-legged with a bead up my nose. It was the missing diamond!

Ivy Randall
b.1909, Blaengarw

The Hall Cinema, Pontycymer 1982.

We used to go to the cinema, see a film and then we'd emulate what we'd seen on the screen. Like, one of us would be Hopalong Cassidy and someone else would be the Lone Ranger and all that nonsense see, and if we could get the costume, mask and things, home-made of course, we were landed.

Bernard Ingram
b.1929, Pontycymer

Perhaps the biggest thrill of those silent-picture days was the serial and the heart-throb Pearl White would have us all on the edge of our seats as an instalment would end with our heroine facing a horrible and certain death which chilled the spine. But, wonder of wonders and to our immense relief, Pearl would miraculously escape for the following Saturday's instalment.

Vernon Chilcott
b.1916, Pontycymer

My favourites was Deanna Durbin films. I was always after her. I was in love with her.

Bill Gibson
b.1920, Ogmore Vale

Wally Carpenter's greatest claim to fame was his orchestra. In the days of silent film there was always a live orchestra in the pit playing music to match the mood of whatever was on the screen at the time. At the old Central Cinema in King Edward Street, the orchestra was led by Wally on the violin, his wife on the piano, and sundry members of his family on the other instruments. Although an original music score always came with the films, which the orchestra was supposed to rehearse beforehand for synchronisation purposes, the Carpenter ensemble rarely bothered to do so. Instead, they had their own stock repertoire like 'I'll see you again' to accompany a tearful parting of lovers. And if the same music was heard week after week throughout the year, somehow it didn't matter.

Grafton Radcliffe
b.1923, Blaengarw

If you met a girlfriend you met in the pictures. You always met in the cinema and you arranged to meet somewhere in the back row, going in seperately. You'd sit in the back row and you'd put your arm around the girl but there was always somebody there in the seat in front like an old deacon or somebody who would see and tell your parents or tell the headmaster and you were caned for it.

Merlin Maddock
b.1934, Pontycymer

Our house was almost opposite the Church Hall and they used to hold dances in there. That was lovely! We used to go - not supposed to of course. The number of times I've been chased out of there for peeping. They weren't sixpenny hops you know, they were upper class dances. Anyway, if you were caught you got a wallop and go home.

Megan Wheeler
b.1921, Blaengarw

Percy Cannon and his Wife, Ogmore Vale c.1930.

I loved to go dancing. 'The Lancers' for one, the two tallest men in the room would come and pick me and my friend 'cause we were the shortest and we'd be swirling around like that - I can still dance now.

Brenda Webster
b.1909, Ogmore Vale

We'd go walking, mountain parading as they called it, on a Sunday. That meant you could walk all the way from Pantygog as far as you wanted, a bunch of boys and a bunch of girls pretending that we are not taking any notice of them, see, and they were pretending they weren't taking any notice of us but it was all a play to get them, I suppose.

Bernard Ingram
b.1929, Pontycymer

We didn't have a lot of opportunities then as teenagers, it was either going up the mountain for walks or nothing. There was nothing much else to do, just walking.

Louise Thomas
b.1909, Ogmore Vale

Promenading, Porthcawl c.1930.

In those days if your brother got married or your sister got married they'd go and live probably in the next street; you didn't go out of the valley.

Charles Bateman
b.1922, Nantymoel

My grandmother was one of the instigators of the revival in Wales in 1905 and Evan Roberts stayed in our house so we had bible for breakfast, bible for dinner, bible for tea, bible for supper, bible every day of the week you know.

Merlin Maddock
b.1934, Pontycymer

We used to have to go to chapel three times every Sunday, course the minister would call in now on a Sunday morning "Have the children gone to chapel?"

Elizabeth Cabble
b.1920, Nantymoel

Sunday School procession, Ogwy Street, Nantymoel c.1900.

Chapels were certainly great promoters of culture... A Cymanfa Ganu was not only a music festival, it became a fashion parade to rival Royal Ascot. Everyone wore a new outfit. For men and boys it was usually a navy-blue serge suit. For the girls and ladies it was a different matter, with a variety of colourful creations (and matching hats) that had come from Morgan Hughes, May Owen's, the Co-op, McAllisters (at a shilling a week), even Stuchberry's and Paris House, Bridgend for the really well-to-do. Another feature of weekday chapel life were the 'Penny Readings'. They were miniature Eisteddfodau in which children and adults competed as singers and elocutionists, always for cash prizes. When a prize was presented to a winner, it was contained in a small velvet bag attached to a sash of ribbon, which was then draped around the victor's neck in much the same way Olympic medals are today. Competition was keen and cut-throat.

Grafton Radcliffe
b.1923, Blaengarw

Blaengarw Trinity English Chapel, c.1900.

82

It was essentially a non-conformist or chapel activity where soloists, elocutionists, writers and storytellers pitted their talents for an audience who had gained admission for tuppence, adults, and one penny for children. These mini-Eisteddfodau would last for hours and were certainly value for money. The musical competitions would embrace solos, duets, quartets, with the adult competitions coming towards the end of the evening, and their prizes sometimes being awarded in a special 'prize bag' made from various materials, artistically decorated, and coveted by prizewinners as much as the actual money won.

Vernon Chilcott
b.1916, Pontycymer

Gwyrosydd (Daniel James) wrote the words of 'Calon Lan' when living at 8 Herbert Street. Tom Bedford Richards of Katie Street set them to music and they were heard for the first time in public at Bethania Chapel.

Grafton Radcliffe
b.1923, Blaengarw

Music class, Ffaldau School c.1954.

Then, again, I think of a man, a very ordinary man. Him and his wife only had one daughter, who died and so he seemed to have used up all his talent in training young boys to play in the Young People's Band. He was a great character. I think the boys stood in awe of him because if you missed practice one day then the next day you could bet that he would be at the school gates waiting for them to bring them to practice. And yet the tremendous respect that was given to this man. I remember when he died and we had a service of remembrance that so many men that came were boys who were taught to play an instrument by band leader Will Evans. Some have gone to music schools, some are playing in many parts of the world really, all through this man who had a great love of teaching the gospel through music.

Gwyneth Lewis
b.1926, Maesteg

Harvest service, Nantymoel c.1930.

Not all were devout Christians. Some went to chapel because it was the thing to do, others for no better reason than it made them feel superior, a few went job-hunting or to preserve the jobs they already had. More jobs were offered and eagerly accepted in chapels than in many an employment exchange.

Grafton Radcliffe
b.1923, Blaengarw

Congregation of Wesley Chapel, Ogmore Vale 1924.

If you were brought up in a chapel and chapel-minded people and people who had businesses, you either mixed with school teachers' sons or policemen's sons or shopkeepers' sons and if you played with other children, you know, you were told off - you weren't supposed to play with them. It's an awful thing to think that I came back here in 1975 and I was talking to a chap he said "I can remember your auntie saying to you," and she was a schoolteacher, "Don't play with those children." Now that's an awful thing for him to remember. I think it's diabolical but it was like that and there was a tremendous amount of sectarianism in the schools regarding this because the teachers obviously knew your father and friends of your father because they were deacons or something in the chapel. The chapel children played together and the other children were different, you know, not different, I mean they played seperately. I find it extremely difficult because some of these miners here spent all the time in an institute reading and were very, very intelligent people and you would converse with them but they didn't rise above that in society, they could never, ever, become a JP. So you had a class of people who are JPs who are telling people how to live and they were living in another - even in a village like this - they lived in another world. I mean, a little village like this to think you had people who thought they were somebody.

Merlin Maddock
b.1934, Pontycymer

Chapel Ministers, Tabernacle, Blaengarw 1920s.

Chapels could be dreadfully narrow-minded. Following evening service there was always a 'gyfeillach' (second meeting). Although gyfeill means friend there was rarely anything friendly about the proceedings. Chapel members were publicly accused of their misdemeanours. I remember a young lady having the finger of scorn pointed at her because she had been seen going to a dance.

Grafton Radcliffe
b.1923, Blaengarw

My grandfather kept The Squirrel, because they kept The Squirrel they weren't allowed to take communion. So the minister would, after church, come around the pub and they'd have communion in the house and then the minister would take home a bottle with him. People used to go around the back of the pub and sit in a place in the back, deacons and various people who were supposed to be non-drinkers go there. Drinking hours were ten o'clock and they'd go at ten past ten when everybody had left and sit around the back.

Merlin Maddock
b.1934, Pontycymer

As a youngster in the Salvation Army you didn't really go to the cinema, so if you went, you went very stealthily making sure that no one saw you. Of course, those kinds of things have long since passed but I can remember if I wanted to see something then we'd have someone on the look-out to make sure that no one from the Army saw us. The Army seems to have been fairly narrow about those kinds of things in the early days but they've moved a long way from there now, for which we are grateful.

Gwyneth Lewis
b.1926, Maesteg

Unknown c.1930.

I suppose one of the striking characters would have been a coloured gentleman who, when you look at his picture anywhere, when it's on display, people will immediately say to you, "Oh, I remember him, he was called Cheerio". I suppose that there's not many people who will know what his real name was. He was Mr. Riley, he beamed. He was a great collector for the Salvation Army. He seemed to have been a striking personality and so well loved and respected.

Gwyneth Lewis
b.1926, Maesteg

Salvation Army Harvest Festival, Ogmore Vale 1932.

87

Sunday School, Tynewydd, Ogmore Vale 1930s.

We were never allowed to read comics or anything on a Sunday. Sunday was Sunday, from the time you got up 'til the time you went to bed it was Sunday. I still feel the same now, I just can't do anything on a Sunday.

Louise Thomas
b.1909, Ogmore Vale

St. Johns Colliery, Maesteg 1980s.

I don't think any of us will ever forget the miners' strike. The terrible sadness involved in this. You see, people are independent really and don't really like to feel that you're giving them a lot of charity and so in a very ordinary way you would try and boost people up and you'll try and do what you can. I think that this is one of the things that we were able to do because a number of our own bandsmen were miners and went through the hardness of the miner's strike and there are still some today who have never been able to get another job. So, I suppose in many ways the Salvation Army, to them, is a haven in more ways than one in that it offers fellowship; it offers many things to them really and it does to anyone who needs it. I think that the Salvation Army has been involved in, perhaps, many things as far as the poorer people are concerned. I can remember as a youngster that the Army served soup in the Junior Hall that we have. I can remember too that the Army has done quite a lot of work here when there was a lot of flooding locally. I can remember too that the Common Market butter that we had was delivered to people and, as far as possible, if there is a need then the Salvation Army will try and meet that need in whatever way or whatever shape it may take.

Gwyneth Lewis
b.1926, Maesteg

I never played, no. I've never taken an interest in sport, never. The only thing I watch is a bit of snooker and that's about all. We used to play that in the hall, in the billiard halls. But anything else, now, I haven't the faintest idea, all I know is one's a round ball and another looking like an egg and that's about it, that's the lot!

Bill Gibson
b.1920, Ogmore Vale

Betws United Rugby Club, 1900s.

I used to play a lot of basket-ball and all that when I was a young lad with the Boys' Club, or rugby, I still play a good game of snooker down in the local club down here, the Non-Political. I enjoy a game. A lot of the boys, most of them are a lot younger than me like but I still enjoy a game. I'm still the president of our darts club, got a darts club, we formed it in 1951.

Charles Bateman
b.1922, Nantymoel

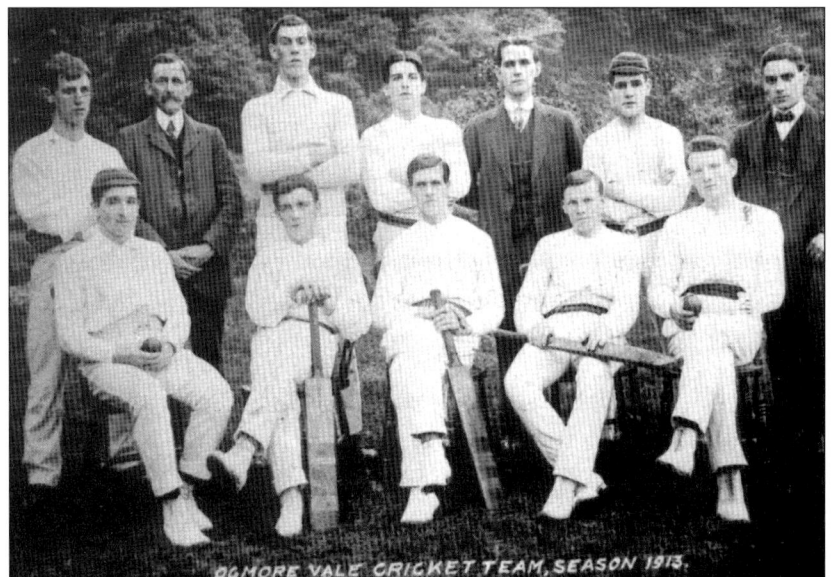

Ogmore Vale Cricket Team, 1913.

What is now Darren Park was once a colliery tip. When Darren Colliery closed men and boys turned it into the playing field it now is. Blaengarw Rugby Club's ground, once a mountain slope, underwent the same transformation. Those who did it had no mechanical diggers and bulldozers, just picks, shovels and plain old-fashioned guts!

Grafton Radcliffe
b.1923, Blaengarw

Levelling out the Darren Tip to make the football field 1930s.

My father had a pig and it used to follow us to school and go back again!

Elizabeth Cabble
b.1920, Nantymoel

We lived in the bottom house in Station Street and down the bottom we had pigs sties and we kept a few pigs, we had chickens. We were well-fed but we had very little money. We, as boys then, was going with a potato sack around certain houses as was keeping the waste and we was collecting them and I always remember you'd have a bag, go to two ot three houses then somebody'd pour a bucket in the bag. Well, when you're carrying that on your back all that be soaking through to your shirt. But we always had, at home, screwed up in the beams, two sides of bacon and the two hams and the two gammons hanging up there just after they'd been salted and you always had that. And for bread, mother used to bake her own. There was two bricks in the pantry, a bit of a plank across and they used to have flour in two hundred pound sacks and you had a sack of flour on the board and then next to it a sack of potatoes. We always had plenty of food in the house.

Station Street, Blaengarw c.1912.

Will Trigg
b.1909, Blaengarw

You had to go to Swansea for the best [lavabread] and my mother was from Swansea, you see, and every time we came on holidays they always made sure I had that. Mike didn't like the look of it but he had a tiny bit and in the end he was as keen as mustard. With bacon, fried, ooh it's gorgeous!

The Strand, Blaengarw c.1910.

Megan Wheeler
b.1921, Blaengarw

Do you know, through my childhood, I never had a Christmas present! The first Christmas present I had was when I was courting my husband and he gave me a box of chocolates. I went in and I put it on the foot of the stairs and when I went up to bed I took it with me and ate the bloody lot!

Brenda Webster
b.1909, Ogmore Vale

As a child, our house - the parlour - there always seemed to be choir practice, either for the chapel or singing for Christmas. Christmas night you wouldn't see my father because and in the quiet of the night, you know, they'd go what they called 'Going round the Rich' which were the doctors, and the teachers, the farmers, they only went around the rich and they went all round the valley down as far as Blackmill singing carols for money. In the quiet of the night you could hear them over in the farm across from us and it used to sort of give a lovely Christmas feeling. You could hear it in the quiet of the night and all Christmas day, then, my father would be flaked out on the bed and then all Christmas then he'd give all us children his share of the money. He had one story, we had a doctor here, Dr. Stewart, he was a Scotchman and he was a character, always (nearly always) drunk but a brilliant doctor. And he said he always remembered, they went to every doctor's house 'cause they was the ones with the money and he was in the front room and the window was open and his legs was hanging out of the window and he said, "Come back tomorrow boys", he was that tight! And do you know, they went back the following day but he gave them a nice sum of money. He was very good.

Margaret Davey
b.1922, Nantymoel

Megan and Arlene Jones, Ogmore Vale,
Christmas 1950s.

Nanymoel Children's Choir (one of the foremost of its time in Wales) with some of the trophies they won, including at least four National Eisteddfod of Wales first prizes c.1924.

I was never aware of poverty. Christmases were always lovely; Father Christmas always came. I didn't know until I was quite big that the lovely toys that we had were made by my father. He was a very good carpenter and he would make us the most beautiful toys; board and easel, hand-made; cots for our dolls, hand-made, beautifully done; a desk; a dresser, a kitchen dresser full of cups and saucers; and always books, they always saw to it that I had books. I always longed to have a train set and never did. There was no boy in our family and in those sexist days it wasn't thought of as a toy for a girl.

Jill John
b.1932, Maesteg

When we were kids, we used to save up our ha'pennies and pennies towards Christmas time and if you looked in the window and you'd seen "That's a shilling," oh well we'd save for that shilling, and believe me it took a long time to save for that shilling for something for Christmas in them days.

Elizabeth Cabble
b.1920, Nantymoel

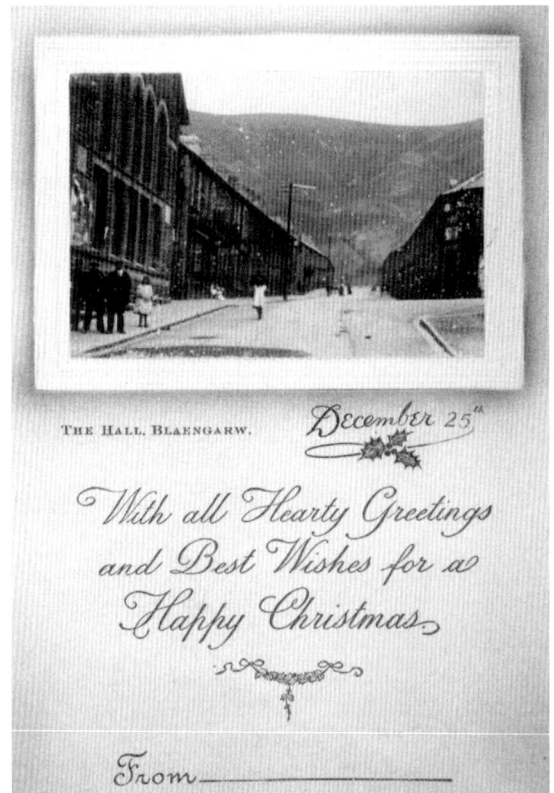

THE HALL, BLAENGARW.

December 25th

With all Hearty Greetings and Best Wishes for a Happy Christmas

From

Christmas Card, Blaengarw c.1920.

Bridge Street, Blaengarw 1981.

98

The Mari Llwyd led by 'Shanco' R Castell, Llangynwyd c.1900.

The new year with the horse, the Mari Llwyd. That was all in Welsh so I didn't understand. It was poetry but by then I had lost my ability to understand a whole lot of his Welsh but the horse would be there with bells and he'd have a drink and a song. We were allowed to stay up for that. He used to come round early, he was an old man and I think when he died I don't think it came but for years before he was around every New Year's Eve.

Megan Wheeler
b.1921, Blaengarw

It's part of the heritage isn't it. Our Hall down here collapsed that year we had the bad rain and they just pulled it down. I'm sorry that it wasn't rebuilt, I think it could have been, see. I don't know what happened but it should have been, it's part of the valley, man.

Bill Gibson
b.1920, Ogmore Vale

Ogmore Vale Workmen's Hall, 1984.

There's been a tremendous loss of culture that was in the valley. We had wonderful culture as children brought up in the valley which my grandchildren, they live in Porthcawl, they've missed out on. Whether life have got a faster pace. Because my son doesn't get home till seven, the men were home by half past three and they'd have a little sleep on the settee then there was always the chapel where you either had drama evenings or you had debating society, you had the children's choirs, you had the Sunday School choirs, we were always taken to somewhere where there was something which was culture, really, which my own grandchildren haven't had. I feel that they've lost out on all that because the only culture they've had is in school. Because the big event was to go to Cardiff to the theatre or an opera, you had to go and see the opera because my father [David Davies] did get an offer to go and join the D'oyly Carte opera but he was a very homesick boy and he went to Cardiff for one term to the school there but he gave it up, he came back.

Margaret Davey
b.1922, Nantymoel

Garw Grammar School, National Eisteddfod 1948.

100

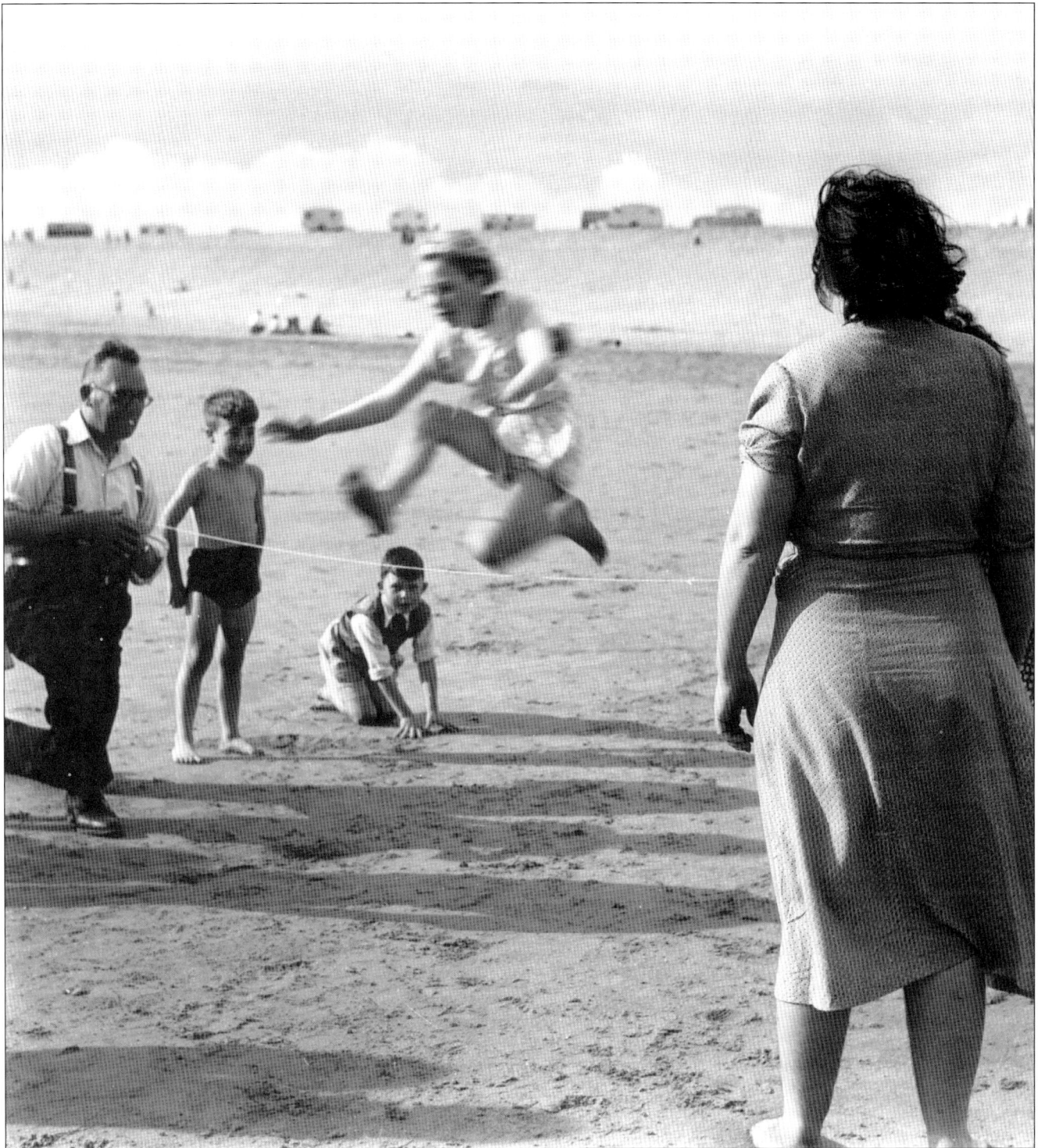

Porthcawl 1950s.

I count myself as being very lucky, I think all my young life was everything that I wanted; loving home, plenty to eat, good advice, strict parents but very caring and taught us right from wrong and I don't think we ever did anything wrong, mainly because I would have got a wallop if I did you know. I had such a nice childhhood. I had a nice growing up and I've had a nice life so, I mean, where do you pick out the good things? I seem to have been lucky enough to have had all the good things.

Megan Wheeler
b.1921, Blaengarw

101

5

"THE PAST IS SECURITY,
THE FUTURE IS ADVENTURE"

Demolition of Wyndham Colliery, Nantymoel 1986.

We haven't rediscovered ourselves yet really, our new identity after iron and coal and the heavy industries when people depended on one another, literally depended on each other, for their lives.

*Jill John
b.1932, Maesteg*

I've lived in Ogmore Vale, we've been married now 52 years but Nantymoel is my home, even now, well, the house I was born in. In fact, I used to go up around there for a walk and see the house where I was born in. I'm quite happy in Ogmore Vale and I've got a lot of friends down here but if I had to say what are you, an Ogmore Vale-ian or a Nantymoel, I am a Nantymoel!

Charles Bateman
b.1922, Nantymoel

Ogmore Vale looking towards Nantymoel 1997.

One brother went to London to live and then my sisters went away but they always come back home, they always loved the valleys.

Elizabeth Roach
b.1921, Nantymoel

Well, the hope that I have is that the younger generation will have more prospects for jobs so that they will have a future in the valley, because once the mines closed there was nothing, well now they have to go to Bridgend and different places to work. I hope that for the future generation that things will get better for them, the job scene. Otherwise, the valley is beautiful, you can live in the valley. On the other hand, if there's no work for the people, it's not encouraging people to come and live in the valley because people want to go where the work is and that's what the younger people will do, I'm afraid. It's more like a residential place, now, on the outskirts that people will live here but travel for their work. There's not much work in the valleys like there used to be.

Elizabeth Roach
b.1921, Nantymoel

Commuter train, Maesteg Station 1995.

It doesn't look nice at all when you see shops just boarded up and left, I'd like to see that cleaned up. I mean, the youngsters of today, they've got a lot of opportunities, we've got a Leisure Centre by here which they can use. That's what I'd like to see, the valley cleaned up a little bit, and them shops, they can't open them but they should be done up, that's one thing I'd like to see.

Charles Bateman
b.1922, Nantymoel

The reclamation scheme is changing the valley the same way as coal changed the valley in the first place. So, we've got another era to look forward to.

Graham Jones,
b.1948, Garw Valley
Bridgend Valleys Railway Society

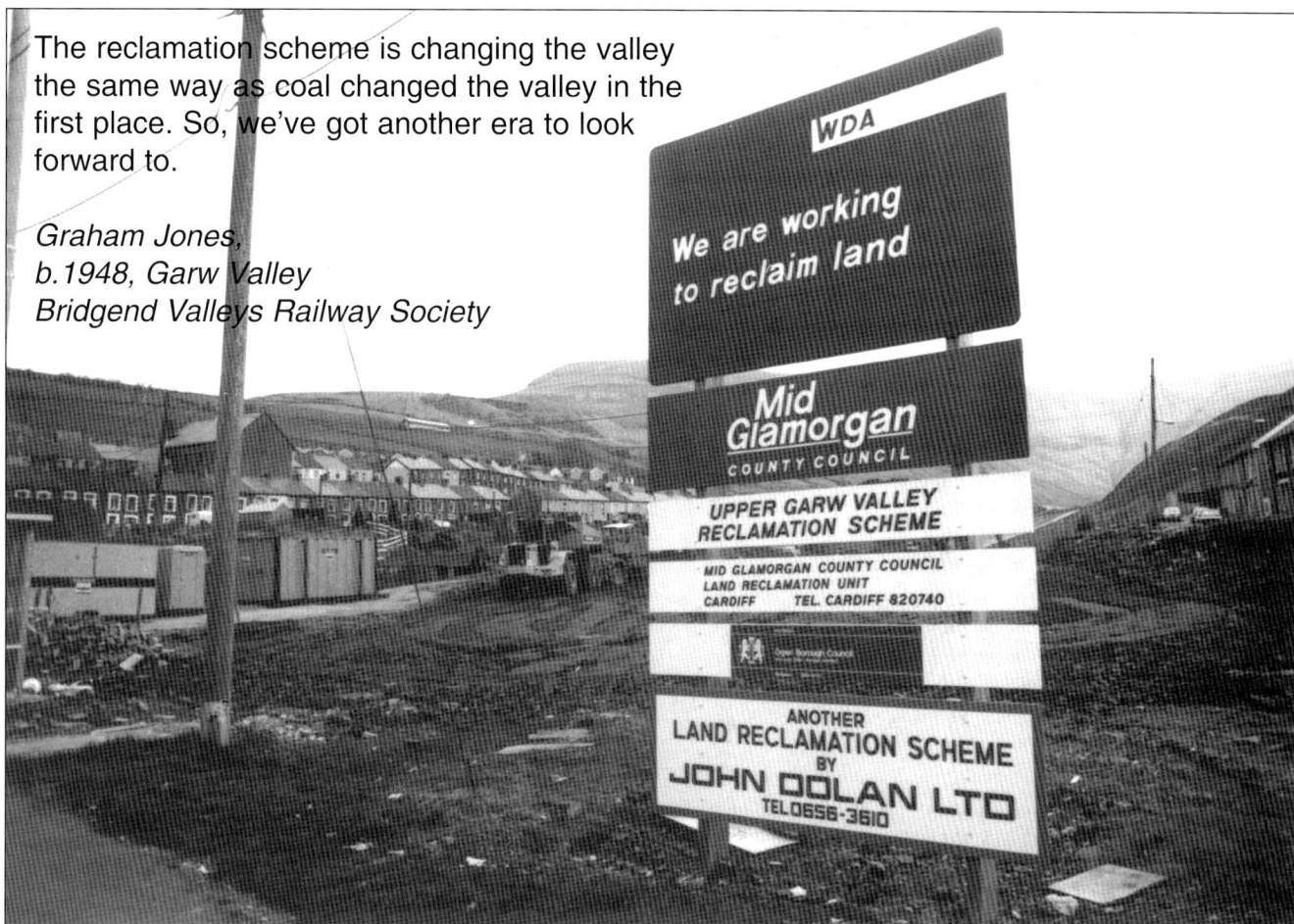

Commencement of Upper Garw Valley reclamation scheme 1988.

Demolition of mine-shaft, Wyndham Colliery, Nantymoel.

Reclamation scheme, Garw Valley 1988.

The comradeship has gone of course but I think the valley's a better place for it mind, it's far prettier than it ever was.

Margaret Davey
b.1922, Nantymoel

Reclamation scheme, Ffaldau Colliery site 1997.

108

I don't think there's another pretty valley in Ogwr I really don't. I mean if people only looked around. I don't understand why people don't come up from Bridgend for a run. I'm sure they're thinking we all live like a lot of higgledy-piggledies because it was a colliery valley like all collieries, but now today it's gorgeous! It's really beautiful!

Ivy Randall
b.1909, Blaengarw

Reclamation scheme, old International Colliery site, Garw Valley 1997.

What I like about the valley is the scenery, the opportunities for various activities to take place up here. It offers a lot to people from outside and it also offers a lot to people inside the valley.

Graham Jones,
b.1948, Garw Valley
Bridgend Valleys Railway Society

A lot of people are moving into the valley. We've had people from the south of England, we've had families moving into the area and they seem to be settling very well and I think that's a hopeful sign.

Jill John
b.1932, Maesteg

To me, Blackmill hasn't changed at all only for more houses built here and private houses over Dan y Coed and posh houses, nice posh bungalows. I don't think anything's really changed, it's just that I'm older.

Gwennie Jones
b.1919, Nantymoel

View of Nantymoel and Ogmore Vale from Pembroke Terrace 1997.

Blaengarw 1997.

I hope for more prosperity for the local people. I hope local people will take more interest in their own valley and to participate more in things that go on in their own valley, not only our generation but the next generation up as well.

Graham Jones,
b.1948, Garw Valley
Bridgend Valleys Railway Society

Nobody, since I've lived here has ever called me Mrs. Jones, never! I like it. Every little child, children up there, I don't know them "Gwennie, hello!" Well, I think 'how do they know my name?'

Gwennie Jones
b.1919, Nantymoel

Katie Street, Blaengarw 1994.

Will Trigg at the Ten Years Without Coal commemorative procession, Garw Valley 1995.

View of bottom lake, Blaengarw 1994.

My hopes are to see from the top lake to the bottom lake like a park and an adventure playground and tennis or bowls - a sporting area for the people and whatever we could do to keep that Hall open for ever and a day. I hope the younger people take heed, this could be a beautiful valley.

Will Trigg
b.1909, Blaengarw

We got to look forward, we can never turn the clock back.

Merlin Maddock
b.1934, Pontycymer

One of the nicest men that I ever had the pleasure of knowing was my father and he was born in Herbert Street in Blaengarw and he gave me such a lot and the only way I can repay him now - and he loved this valley and he came back and his ashes are in the Garw Fechan - and the only way I can repay him was by working hard for where he loved so much.

Councillor Wayne Sherlock
b.1940, Blaengarw

Pontyrhyl and Garw Fechan 1997.

Since I've not been well, it's the first time last Saturday that I walked up over the top and I managed it with two stops, up to where the aerial was, and I walked down Garw Fechan. Half way down I saw - I don't know how many in Pontycymer have seen it - I saw a green and yellow (yellow back, green belly) woodpecker, *brr - brr,* like a pneumatic drill, you know, going off. The thing about a woodpecker is brilliant, you see him on the tree hitting the tree then as soon as he sees you he doesn't fly away he walks in a spiral around the back of the tree and he does this - grips the tree. He actually walks up a tree like as if he's got magnetic boots on you know. He's there, *brr,* like a motorbike going away and then he gradually, step by step, he disappears around the back and he will not come from there. You can go where you want to, I've got these little binoculars and I go and hide, he knows you are there you can't see him again. I think that's lovely.

Merlin Maddock
b.1934, Pontycymer

Walkers resting on the Community Route, Nantymoel 1997.

A community route is to run parallel with the railway and walkers can come up or down the line, either on the train or on the cycle track. The basic plans at the moment are to run, probably, steam on a weekend; I should think the first train will be diesel due to the availability of rolling stock and of engines. Eventually, we're hoping to run a community service from here to Tondu every day to take people to work as well as being used as a tourist attraction. It can bring people up here to use the cycle track, use all the facilities and the other things that have been started up here it will be sort of the lifeline for the Garw. With the hill walks as well it's going to be quite an exciting time, for everybody.

Graham Jones,
b.1948, Garw Valley
Bridgend Valleys Railway Society

I think it's great for the children and for the grown-ups, they've all got their bikes and they're up and down, it's lovely, they're coming up and down and half-way down this part of the cycle track they're starting to make a wetlands. I think it's a project with the local council and I think it's wonderful. The more they involve the children, the more the children will look after these things, and it's starting to be that way you know.

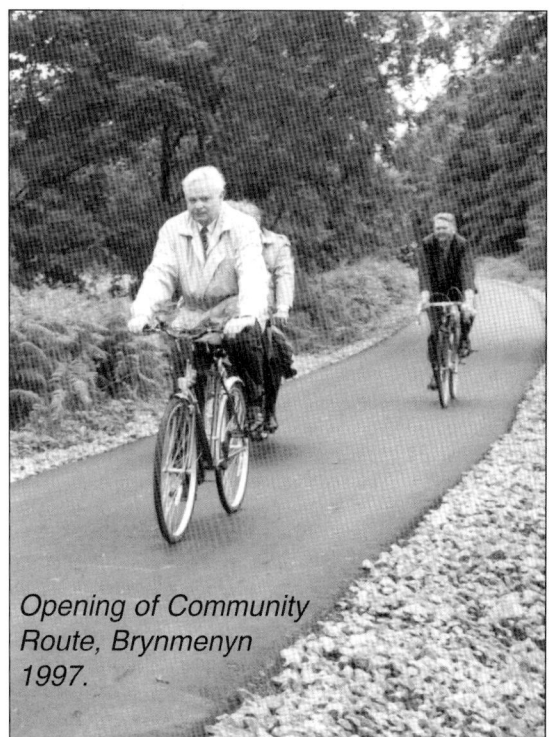

Opening of Community Route, Brynmenyn 1997.

Charles Bateman
b.1922, Nantymoel

115

This is potentially a most beautiful area in which to live, has a lot to offer... We're definitely cleaner in many ways, the air is cleaner. Maesteg is a very nice place to live, there's a whole range of entertainment and culture, there's a lot going on.

Jill John
b.1932, Maesteg

Maesteg Town Centre 1997.

The buzzards and crows - we've got peregrine falcons here which people travel to see. We've got the dippers in the river and up on the mountainside, there's various birds up there and we've even seen a squirrel around here recently. We've even heard rumours that there are otters further down the river.

Ian Read
b.1961, Blaengarw

Llynfi Valley from Croeserw 1997.

It's got prettier, it's got so much prettier. As children we roamed these mountains, it was nothing to walk to the top, go right across from the Bwlch to the 'Sugar Loaf' and come back down this end. That was nothing, but of course you can't leave children like that now, it's not safe.

Margaret Davey
b.1922, Nantymoel

Peregrine Falcon, Garw Valley 1996.

Lluest Colliery ruins and Pontyrhyl 1996.

The summers seemed to be longer when I was younger, there seemed to be finer weather, you know. But we, a lot of children, used to go up on the mountain and have picnics. That doesn't happen anymore. Perhaps it is my imagination, but the summers seemed to be warmer and nicer and the children used to play and have picnics.

Elizabeth Roach
b.1921, Nantymoel

Bathers by the lake, Blaengarw 1997.

It seems to be nothing now to be announcing somebody's age. We usually talk about their birthdays. You often now are announcing the fact that people are well past eighty and so it is the fact that people are living much longer. When I was a child forty was old. Yes, I can remember thinking that forty was old.

Gwyneth Lewis
b.1926, Maesteg

Valley and Vale Summer Scheme Photography Group 1997.

What is so pleasurable is that when you are on top of the mountain and you're sitting down there and you look down the valley and think of all the older generation, they're all up in boot hill up the cemetary there, all those men have toiled their whole lives to put all that coal up there, now it's all being brought back down to make it look nice, you know, and pleasant, and hopefully it will look very pleasant, I think. I look at that and while you are up there what you hear 'da da da da da da da da da' ["We'll keep a welcome in the hillside"], bloody ice -cream van. So I'm glad to get over the top in the Garw Fechan where I can hear a river. I think that is the end, the end, if it you sit up there and think 'God my grandfather was here, my great grandfather was here, we all went to the school' and you hear 'da da da da da da da da da,' and you just go over the hillside and you hear the river running down, hear the birds. That to me is a lovely place, I can sit there for hours.

Merlin Maddock
b.1934, Pontycymer.

My sister in law, she's eighty three, she's been picking wimberries now recently. People do go picking wimberries and blackberries and things, there are a lot of wimberries up in the mountains but the weather used to be nicer to go and pick them.

Elizabeth Roach
b.1921, Nantymoel

Site of the old Caerau Colliery, Llynfi Valley 1997.

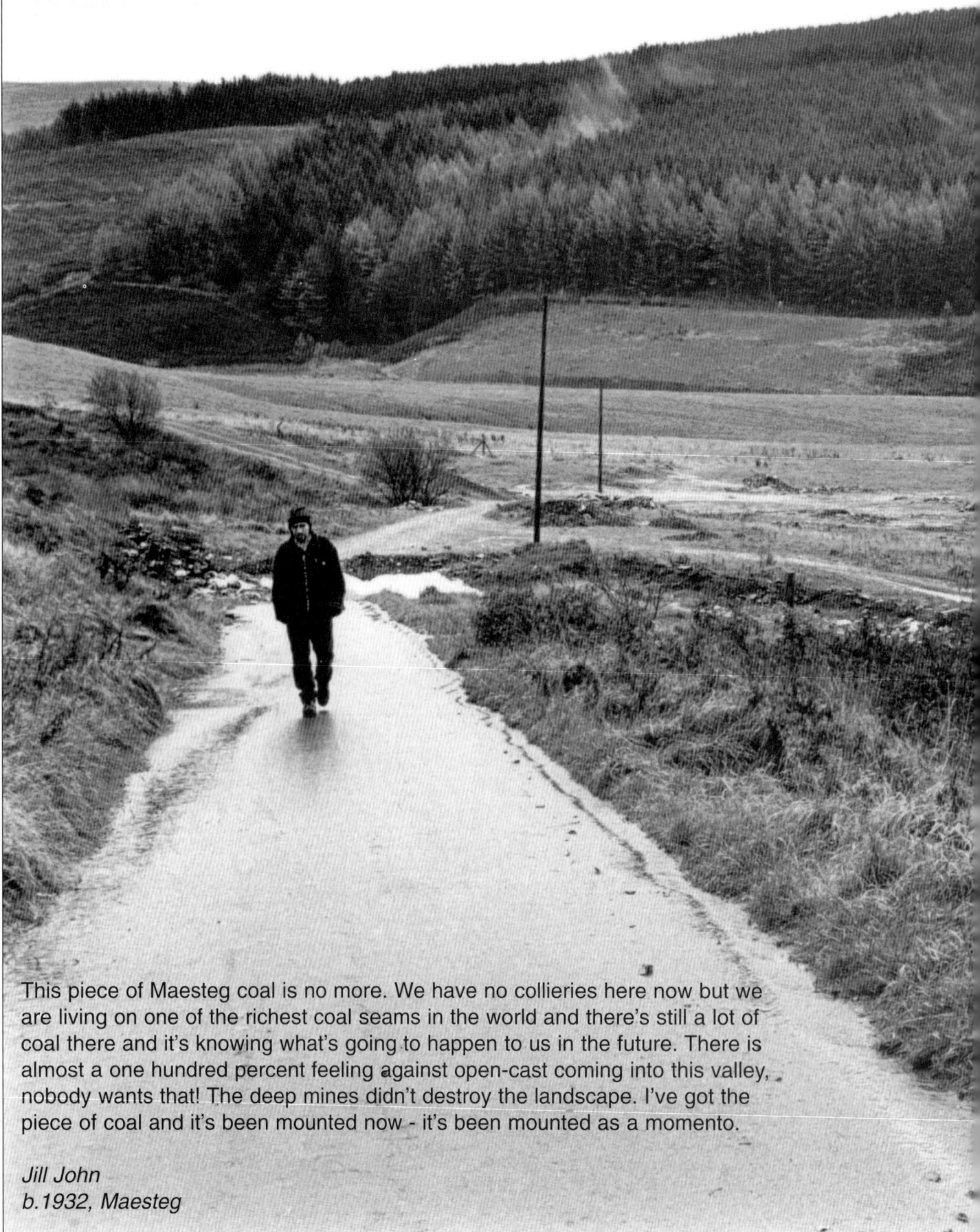

This piece of Maesteg coal is no more. We have no collieries here now but we are living on one of the richest coal seams in the world and there's still a lot of coal there and it's knowing what's going to happen to us in the future. There is almost a one hundred percent feeling against open-cast coming into this valley, nobody wants that! The deep mines didn't destroy the landscape. I've got the piece of coal and it's been mounted now - it's been mounted as a momento.

Jill John
b.1932, Maesteg

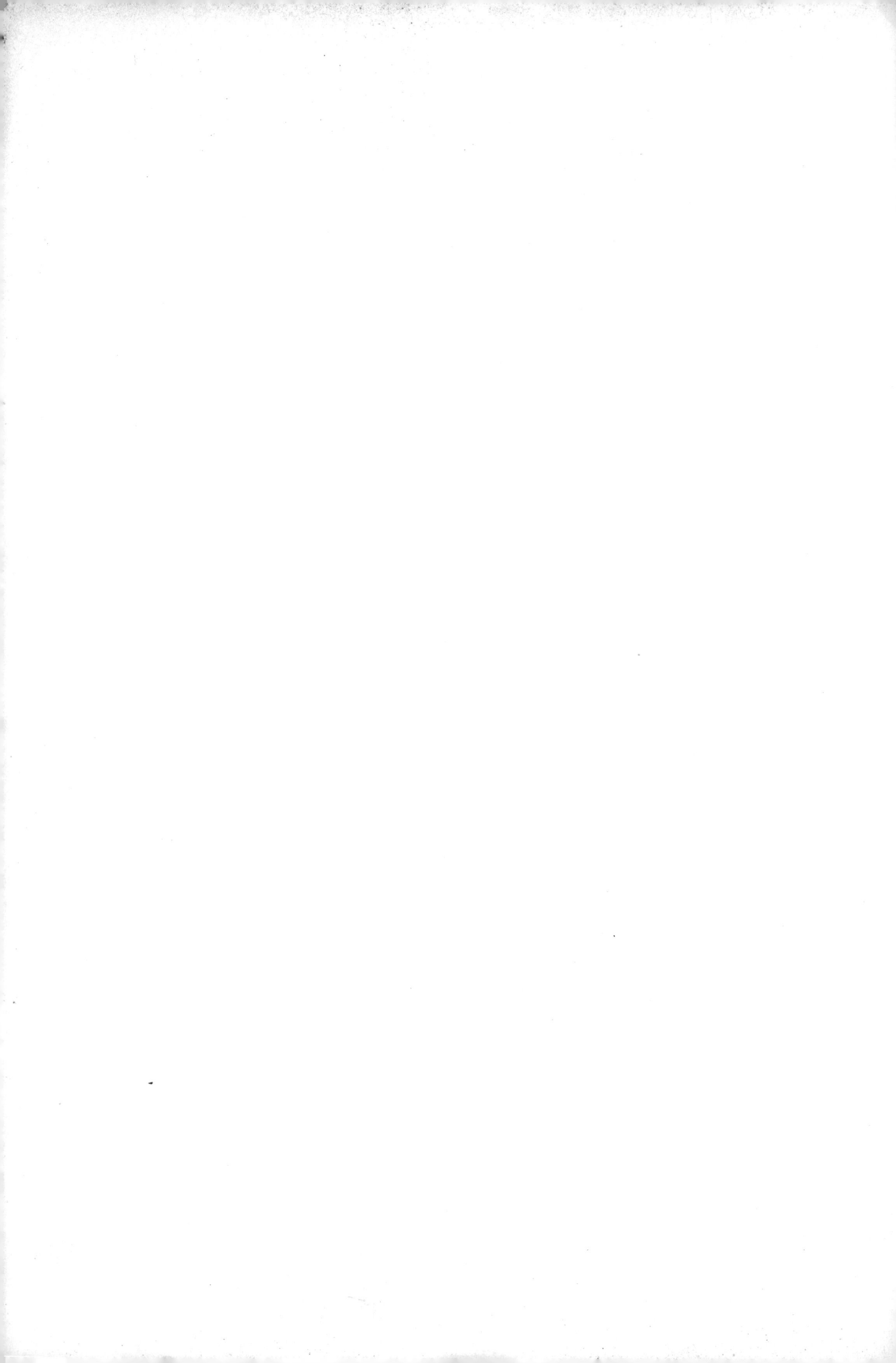